PRAISE FOR REDRAWING THE BLUEPRINTS FOR THE EARLY CHURCH

“Bringing fresh insights to the history of restorationist theology, John Young illustrates the flexibility of restorationism as he teases out comparable patterns within fellowships not often compared. With an engaging writing style, he contributes to the scholarly investigation of the restoration principle and promotes self-reflection within congregations of the Stone-Campbell Movement. Personally invested in the task, Dr. Young is at the outset of a promising career of professional service to the church.”

— John C. Hardin, Museum Division Director
Alabama Department of Archives and History

"Those within the Stone-Campbell Movement have traditionally been united in a desire to restore the early church. But what exactly does that mean? John Young shows that a commitment to restoration has taken various forms inside and outside the SCM. His analysis provides perspective, humility, and greater understanding to those who see restoration and unity as goals worth pursuing."

—John Bradford, Preaching Minister
Prairie Grove Church of Christ

“Among the numerous strengths of Young’s analysis are its comparative approach and focus on the margins. By comparing four unique restorationist groups, which are either on the fringes of Stone-Campbell studies and thus often overlooked in mainstream histories or are too new to have a developed historiography, Young is able to chart new terrain, highlight commonalities and differences among diverse restorationist conceptions of the ancient church, and point to prospective paths of exploration. Young's insightful use of 'historical ecclesiology' as an analytical category fosters exploration of restorationist themes including the nature of the Bible, determination of the temporal bounds of the normative church, complexities of determining the content and process of replicating the ancient church, and 'recursive' restorationism's propensity to idealize its own origins and early leaders as worthy of emulation. Young's comparative and thematic approach offers rich resources to American religious historians and scholars of restorationism."

—James L. Gorman, Professor of History
Johnson University

"With a scholar's eye and a storyteller's voice, John Young crafts a masterfully illuminating narrative of the breadth and durability of restorationism as an organizing framework in American Christianity. Shattering the traditional dichotomies of 'exclusive or inclusive' and 'primitivist or modernist' that dominate Stone-Campbell Movement studies, Young presents an 'historical ecclesiology' that is both malleable and pervasive across the traditions he explores. Objective yet incisive, wide-ranging yet cohesive, *Redrawing the Blueprints for the Early Church* is a story of restorationist Christianity that desperately needs to be read and taught by students and scholars of American religion."

—Corey Markum, Assistant Professor of History
Freed-Hardeman University

REDRAWING THE BLUEPRINTS FOR THE EARLY CHURCH

HISTORICAL ECCLESIOLOGY IN AND AROUND THE STONE-CAMPBELL MOVEMENT

JOHN YOUNG

Redrawing the Blueprints for the Early Church
Historical Ecclesiology in and around the Stone-Campbell Movement

Published by Heritage Christian University Press

Manufactured in the United States of America

Cataloging-in-Publication Data

John Young, 1989–
Redrawing the blueprints for the early church: historical ecclesiology in and around the Stone-Campbell Movement / by John Young

p. cm.

Includes index.

ISBN 978-1-7347665-7-8 (pbk.); 978-1-7347665-8-5 (e-book)

1. Restoration movement (Christianity). 2. Christadelphians. 3. International Churches of Christ. 4. Christian Church (Disciples of Christ). 5. Non-institutional churches. 6. Emerging Church movement—United States. I. Author. II. Title.

BX7077 .Y68 2021 286.6—dc20

Library of Congress Control Number: 2020924040

Cover design by Brad McKinnon and Brittany VanderMaas

CONTENTS

ACKNOWLEDGMENTS

Given how closely connected this book is to its predecessor (and sort-of companion) volume *Visions of Restoration: The History of Churches of Christ*, which happily emerged from the same batch of doctoral research, I thought it might be fitting to just have a footnote here leading you back to the acknowledgments section from that first book. I am a historian, after all.[1]

For the sake of completeness, though, I would also need to point you toward the acknowledgments section of the dissertation which served as the basis for this work, as I'm indebted to many other people whose contributions were not mentioned specifically in the previous book.[2]

The less-glib truth is that as I sit here in February 2021, I have been working on this project in some form or fashion since October 2015. (That was when I started writing an end-of-the-semester research paper on the Christadelphians for a graduate seminar in religious history.) In the intervening five-plus years, I have accumulated a score of debts to librarians, archivists, editors, readers, listeners, reviewers, professors, mentors, colleagues, friends, and family members, each of whom has in some way, large or small, contributed to the successes of the volume you now hold in your hands. If you think you fall into one of those categories, you probably do, and I thank you for it. If you're not sure, pick the one that seems closest and know that I thank you for your help, too. And even if you don't think you contributed anything or are due any thanks from me, I thank you for (if nothing else!) humoring me by making it this far down the page. Keep reading, and I hope what follows will be a blessing to you.

NOTES TO ACKNOWLEDGMENTS

1. John Young, *Visions of Restoration: The History of Churches of Christ* (Florence, AL: Cypress Publications, 2019), vii-ix.

2. John Young, "Redrawing the 'Blueprints' for the Early Church: Historical Ecclesiology in and around the Stone-Campbell Movement" (PhD diss., the University of Alabama, 2020), v-vi.

REDRAWING THE BLUEPRINTS FOR THE EARLY CHURCH

FOREWORD

I recall attending a Church of Christ in my young adulthood and noticing at the bottom corner of the building a stone that read "Founded A.D. 30." At the time, I did not understand the message communicated by that stone—the belief that all historical events between Christ's death and the founding the ministry of Barton Stone and Alexander Campbell in the early nineteenth century (or even the founding of that particular congregation) had no relevance to the identity of the movement that took their name. Early followers of Stone and Campbell often viewed the movement as "ahistorical" or outside of history. Their embrace of "restorationism" (restoring the patterns of the early church in the modern era) set them on a path of rejecting all "Christian" history as the story of manmade religion, not God's movement among people. After spending over two decades studying the Stone-Campbell Movement, I have come to recognize the complex relationship between the Churches of Christ and the study of history. Throughout much of its history, the movement rejected "denominationalism" as humans corrupting the church and to the extent that "church history" reflected the story of denominationalism it too had little relevance. Thus, many members believed the Churches of Christ were something new that had no history save that written in the Bible (hence the "Founded A.D. 30" label on the cornerstone of many churches). With this attitude toward human history, it is little wonder that until the past few decades, unlike most other Christian traditions, the Stone-Campbell Movement only produced a few (though notable) historians.[1]

Despite the movement's rejection of historical study in the early years of its development, recent decades have seen growing interest in exploring the historical forces acting upon founders and members of Stone-Campbell churches. The 2004 *Encyclopedia of the Stone-Campbell Movement* and the 2013 *The Stone-Campbell Movement: A Global History* reflect the growing attention to the historical interpretation of the movement.[2] A new generation of scholars have even more recently extended the focus into a wide array of historical issues such as James Gorman, Jeff Childers, and Mark Hamilton's work on slavery, Tanya Smith Brice's work on race relations in Churches of Christ, and my work on women and gender in the Stone-Campbell Movement.[3]

John Young's *Redrawing the Blueprints for the Early Church: Historical Ecclesiology in and around the Stone-Campbell Movement* furthers the expanding influence of this younger generation of Stone-Campbell Movement scholars. He documents how different traditions within and adjacent to the Stone-Campbell Movement have engaged the project of restorationism (and thus engaged history) differently. Young's project enlarges upon the work of Doug Foster, Richard Hughes and others who have centralized the role of restorationism in the development of the Stone-Campbell Movement. *Redrawing the Blueprints for the Early Church* examines how various traditions within the Stone-Campbell Movement have not so much rejected history as they have redefined the eras of history that matter most. Thus, the Stone-Campbell Movement is not ahistorical but instead selectively focused on particular eras of the past and their meaning for the present (especially the experiences of the first century church as depicted in the New Testament). However, this project of restoring the early church has itself been a more challenging journey than the movement's first generation may have appreciated, a key focus in Young's study. Approaches to restorationism itself can also be shaped by the experiences and contexts of those who have engaged upon it.

Young's investigation of how implementing the model offered by the first century Christian church was pursued by Stone-Campbell churches adds several concepts that advance a deeper understanding of restorationism. For instance, he adopts the term "recursion" to describe how later generations appended the theology and practice of the first generation of Stone-Campbell preachers to what may need restoration in contemporary churches. Thus, many churches engage not only in restoring the first century church but also the practices early preachers established in the movement that may have subsequently been eroded or lost. In this and other interpretations, he brings the fresh perspectives of a new generation of Stone-Campbell scholars who are enlarging our understandings of the complexity of the movement's past and present.

Young's project succeeds most in revealing the complexities of restorationism and its influence on Stone-Campbell history through the lens of traditions that do not often receive the focus of historical investigation. He puts four traditions (the Christadelphians, the Emerging Church Movement, the International Churches of Christ, and non-institutional Churches of Christ) into conversation with one another. The various approaches of these traditions yield insight into the different interpretations of restorationism and the difficulty of replicating the early church in the current era. Each encountered their own challenges in achieving a vision of restoring the early church. Understanding how they experienced these challenges differently and responded with divergent theologies and practices uncovers the central intricacies of the Stone-Campbell Movement itself.

With the addition of Young's work to the scholarship on the Stone-Campbell Movement, historians will find a deeper engagement with the historical significance of restorationism. In this, Young has made a valuable contribution to the emerging scholarship on the history of this tradition.

Loretta Long Hunnicutt
Pepperdine University
December 2020

NOTES TO FOREWORD

1. One important exception is the Christian Church (Disciples of Christ) stream of the movement which maintained a greater degree of interest in history and thus produced much of the history of the movement that was available until recent interest has grown in other parts of the movement.

2. Douglas A. Foster et al, *The Encyclopedia of the Stone-Campbell Movement: Christian Church (Disciples of Christ), Christian Churches/Churches of Christ/Churches of Christ* (Grand Rapids, MI: Eerdmans, 2004); D. Newell Williams, Douglas A Foster, and Paul M Blowers, *The Stone-Campbell Movement: A Global History* (St. Louis: Chalice, 2013).

3. See James L. Gorman, Jeff Childers, and Mark Hamilton, editors, *Slavery's Long Shadow: Race and Reconciliation in American Christianity* (Grand Rapids, MI: Eerdmans, 2019); Tanya Smith Brice, editor, *Reconciliation Reconsidered: Advancing the National Conversation on Race in Churches of Christ* (Abilene, TX: Abilene Christian University Press, 2016); Loretta Hunnicutt, "What I learned About Women," *Stone-Campbell Journal* 16:1 (Fall 2013) and "Freedom to Speak, Freedom to Serve: Women's Changing Roles in the Stone-Campbell Movement," *Christian History Magazine* Issue 106 (Fall 2013).

INTRODUCTION

RESTORATION

In a 1995 editorial in the *Journal of Church and State*, religious historian Edwin S. Gaustad wrote, not without reason, that "a great many citizens of the United States have a limited awareness or appreciation of history." Such ignorance and apathy were not limited to Gaustad's own era, of course. Some of the all-time worst offenders in these regards, he continued, had been the restorationist Christians of the nineteenth century frontier. For them, "True religion consisted in returning to that Golden Age, ignoring everything that had obscured and encrusted the pure Christianity of the first century." No great lovers of the past for its own sake, Gaustad's restorationists "were prepared to treat history lightly, if not disdainfully."[1] Their primitivist faith, Mark A. Noll agreed elsewhere, "sought to dispense with history almost entirely in its effort to recapture the pristine glories of New Testament Christianity."[2]

Gaustad and Noll are quite right that these primitivist

pioneers devoted themselves to restoring the version of Christianity they deemed to be correct—namely, the faith of the first century church. But the two historians err in assuming that the restorationists had little regard for the past as a whole. While early Disciples did describe the Bible "as an inviolate, timeless source of truth," religion scholar Seth Perry notes, they were also keenly aware of the physical impacts of editing, translation, and related processes on actual biblical texts. Likewise, he contends, viewing the restorationists' romanticization of the first century church as an Eliadean conceptualization of sacred time is to miss the point entirely: "For early Disciples, the Bible did not concern an exemplary past outside of time, but rather documented specific, historically and geographically locatable, and avowedly irrepeatable events."[3]

The writings of the nineteenth century restorationists, as well as those of their twentieth- and twenty-first-century progeny, undoubtedly contain their fair share of factual errors, logical fallacies, methodological mess-ups, and questionable conclusions. Yet for all of these shortcomings, the restorationist project is inherently historical because it necessarily involves examining sources from and about the past and drawing conclusions in the present based on those readings.[4] This is not to say that restorationists have all been professionally trained historians—though they have been strongly represented in certain corners of the discipline, at least.[5] Rather, the point is that restorationism by definition requires reading sources from the past and drawing conclusions from and about them in the present day.

There can be, of course, major differences between the historical endeavors of restorationist Christians and those of unaffiliated academic historians using modern methods. Not all professionals would give such unquestioning deference to the Acts of the Apostles or to other New Testament texts as historical sources, nor are their projects as likely to be guided by explicitly theological goals, such as the recovery of proper doctrine for use in the present day. Yet even though the attempt to return present-day Christianity to a first century model does require a running leap over centuries and centuries of later Christian history, the attempt is only undertaken because of two implicit historical assumptions: first, that there was something qualitatively different about the earliest era of the Christian faith compared to later generations; and second, that that "something" changed or disappeared as time progressed. Additionally, while the language used by restorationists to express their historical thinking often differs from that used by professional historians, the lack of discipline-specific terminology does not indicate a lack of discipline-specific thought. Somewhat ironically, it is the professional historians, not the amateurs, who have been slower to grasp this point.[6]

That restorationism is inherently historical in nature is a key thrust of this book, but an equally significant point is that restorationists' beliefs about the early church have histories of their own, varying as they have over time and from group to group.[7] Understanding the diversity of restorationist outcomes can best be accomplished, I believe, by carefully examining what restorationist Christians have said about the early church and then divining the "blueprints" which they must have been using, whether consciously or unconsciously, to guide their respective restoration projects.

As a shorthand expression which means, in essence, a restorationist group's conceptions of the early church at a given time in that group's history, I am employing the term "historical ecclesiology." I am certainly not the first scholar to use the phrase "historical ecclesiology," though the meaning I attach to it is different from its previous uses. For example, in 2004, the Catholic theologian Roger Haight published the first volume of his sweeping *Christian Community in History*, subtitled *Historical Ecclesiology*. In the work, Haight, following the lead of Edward Schillebeeckx,[8] sought to outline an "ecclesiology from below" for the modern church, a historical ecclesiology rooted in the experiences and contexts of its past members:

> It is not the case that an ecclesiology from below renders theological interpretation dependent upon some particular social reconstruction. It is rather the case that just as God's Word was incarnate in Jesus, so that to encounter God there one must turn to that history, so that to understand God's action in forming the church one must attend to that history.[9]

Neil Ormerod has undertaken a similar effort in his *Re-Visioning the Church: An Experiment in Systematic-Historical Ecclesiology*, arguing that "the goal of ecclesiology is bringing together an upper blade that incorporates the social sciences with the lower blade of a narrative of the history of the Church."[10] While each of these works contributes usefully to historical and theological conversations about the church, their authors seek a very different end than I do here. Whereas Schillebeeckx, Haight, Ormerod, and other theologians have turned to the church of the past to formulate a vision for the church of the present and future, I am looking to the church of the recent past to recover what believers have thought about the church of the more distant past.

I have relied on a variety of primary sources, primarily (though not exclusively) published print materials, in reconstructing my groups' historical ecclesiologies. My aim in giving greater precedence to formally published sources is, somewhat paradoxically, to get as close as possible to how the imaginary "average group member" would have thought about the early church. To be sure, many, even most, of the authors whose works I cite were prominent figures in their respective movements; my sources are not necessarily representative in that regard. But while it is incorrect to assume that church members always toe the party line on all points of theology, I do believe that official and quasi-official books, newspapers, tracts, podcasts, plays, movies, and blog posts reflect and shape widely shared beliefs—even if no other individual in a movement believed precisely the same things as the creator of a particular work.

Aside from highlighting the historical impulse within restorationism and introducing the concept of historical ecclesiology, chapters one, three, and four of this work also continue the recent expansion of Restoration, or Stone-Campbell, Movement studies beyond the "Big Three" groups—Disciples of Christ, independent Christian Churches, and Churches of Christ—by telling the stories of three smaller fellowships on the margins of the movement.[11] Additionally, chapter two makes the case that the recent Emerging Church Movement, notwithstanding its post-modern skepticism of received tradition, has been powerfully shaped by a modified form of restorationist theology.[12] Bringing these four groups together into one volume helps illustrate that restorationist Christians can be, and have been, united in restorationist *motivations* even while being quite divided in their restorationist *outcomes*, in turn offering a new perspective on the age-old "restoration vs. unity" theme in the movement's historiography.[13]

THE ONGOING WIDENING OF STONE-CAMPBELL MOVEMENT STUDIES

In broadest terms, the recent trend within Stone-Campbell Movement historiography has been toward a wider lens and more inclusive portrait, moving beyond initial interpretations which saw the Disciples of Christ as the true heirs of the movement and other groups, particularly Churches of Christ, as troublesome offshoots hardly worthy of historical consideration.[14] While there have long been high-quality academic studies of the various fellowships, most of these earlier works focused exclusively on one group or another, with varying amounts of regard for what might have been happening concurrently in the other fellowships.[15] In 2004, however, the publication of the *Encyclopedia of the Stone-Campbell Movement* offered a strong challenge to this historiographical separation by bringing together scholars and scholarship from nearly all corners of the movement. The work's editors hailed from each of the "Big Three" traditions, and its articles covered an even broader swath of fellowships.[16] The *Encyclopedia* proved to be a powerful step toward a more inclusive history of the Stone-Campbell Movement. In 2013, another massive undertaking, *The Stone-Campbell Movement: A Global History*, took up the challenge laid down by the editors of the *Encyclopedia* (three of whom would oversee this later volume also) to expand the story of the movement beyond North America to include voices and perspectives from Stone-Campbell fellowships around the world.[17]

This book aims to build on these and related efforts by taking as its subjects three fellowships (the Christadelphians, the non-institutional Churches of Christ, and the International Churches of Christ) which still remain on the fringes of Stone-Campbell studies,[18] as well as a more recent Christian group (the Emerging Church Movement) which evinces several notable similarities to the early SCM.[19] These four groups were not selected entirely for novelty's sake, though I do believe that there is value in the simple act of bringing their stories together. Rather, I have chosen to focus on them because their respective historical ecclesiologies help illustrate (1) the flexibility of restorationist theology, both inside and outside of the movement; and (2) the reality that restorationist theology is by its very definition a historical undertaking, whether or not the history undergirding it always meets modern professional standards.

Additionally, emphasizing the connections between my featured groups and the "Big Three" Stone-Campbell fellowships will hopefully allow for greater cross-pollination between their scholarly literatures, which all have much to contribute but which have often been walled off from one another. While important scholarship has been done on all four of these groups, relatively little of that work has been crafted by historians, and even those fractions which are have tended to speak within their own separate historiographical conversations.

HISTORIOGRAPHY OF CHRISTADELPHIANISM

Foremost of the few scholarly books on the Christadelphian movement is Bryan R. Wilson's *Sects and Society: A Sociological Study of Three Religious Groups in Britain.*[20] In *Sects and Society*, Wilson seeks to explain how members of the Elim Tabernacle, Christian Science, and Christadelphianism had resisted the temptation to attenuate their more countercultural aspects in response to generational changes and pressures from the secularizing world around them.[21] That these "sects" could maintain their identity went against the prevailing wisdom of the era.[22] Scholars of American sectarianism, for instance, had found that such groups almost universally made the transition to full-fledged denominations, at peace with wider Christendom, by their second or third generation. No less a luminary than H. Richard Niebuhr even suggested that a sect "by its very nature... is valid only for one generation."[23]

How, then, did Wilson's three case studies buck the trend? Wilson argues that Britain's internal migration patterns during the nineteenth and twentieth centuries ensured a steady flow of job-seekers into the urban areas which constituted the three sects' geographical strongholds. Displaced from their traditional ways of life, and set adrift in cities full of similarly disconnected people, such workers turned to demanding religious groups, like the Christadelphians, in an attempt to bring a sense of community to their lives. These newcomers' voluntary allegiance meant that the sects were "always a first-generation experience for some," and as such were able to retain their original missions. For the Christadelphians in particular, this meant the preservation of their adventism, which they indirectly inherited from the teachings of William Miller.[24]

Although Wilson's analysis in *Sects and Society* continues to guide academic study of Christadelphianism to this day, only one third of his book focuses on the movement, and Christadelphian history is confined to a single chapter.[25] Charles H. Lippy's *The Christadelphians in North America*, the second major scholarly work covering the group, was actually the first to be devoted wholly to Christadelphianism.[26] Lippy begins by reconstructing the spiritual origins of the movement, showing how evangelical revivals, Scottish "common sense" philosophy, millennialism, and anti-Catholicism together constituted the American religious milieu in which Christadelphianism was born.[27] From there, he devotes a chapter to the life of Christadelphian founder John Thomas, and a chapter to subsequent developments in the group's history through the late 1980s.

Like Wilson's *Sects and Society*, Lippy's work draws from a variety of academic disciplines, and only the first three chapters of the book describe the history of Christadelphianism per se. (Later sections include deep dives into the movement's theology, sociology, and impact on the broader story of American religion.) His analysis places great significance on Thomas and his idiosyncratic version of the Christian faith, countering Wilson's assertion that "the history of the Christadelphian movement is only in its very early stages the history of its founder, Dr. John Thomas."[28] Broadly speaking, though, the two scholars' works complement each other quite well, given their distinct geographical areas of concern, and Wilson himself gave high praise to *The Christadelphians in North America* upon its release.[29]

The most recent of the three key scholarly books on Christadelphian history is the only one to have been written by a member of the group. In 1997, Andrew R. Wilson (no apparent relation to the earlier Wilson) published *The History of the Christadelphians, 1864-1885: The Emergence of a Denomination*, an expansion of his master's thesis, which was originally undertaken because of Wilson's admitted lack of knowledge about the history of his own tradition.[30] Acknowledging the importance of John Thomas to the history of Christadelphianism, Wilson nevertheless persuasively contends that "there was no monolithic consistency about [his] theological writings," and that it was left to Thomas's successor, Robert Roberts, to create "from the chaos a neat, well-oiled machine that ticked over nicely."[31]

Wilson chooses as his starting date Roberts's July 1864 promotion to the editorship of the movement's leading periodical, the *Ambassador of the Coming Age* (later, the *Christadelphian*); at that time, he argues, Roberts "was elevated... from being *primus inter pares* to being *primus*" among Christadelphians.[32] As had Bryan R. Wilson three decades earlier, Andrew R. Wilson portrays Roberts as a generally effective leader, if not an overly original thinker.[33] For all of Roberts's successes, however, in the areas of evangelism, intra-movement communication, and organization, Wilson notes with more than a touch of regret that the 1885 schism over resurrectional responsibility[34] might have been avoided if either Thomas or Roberts had given greater attention to matters of church governance: "On the rock of failures in that area, the ship of success foundered in 1884-1885, and much of the precious cargo was lost."[35] Despite its significantly narrower chronological window, Wilson's work dwarfs both *Sects and Society* and *The Christadelphians in North America* in both page count and minute historical detail.

HISTORIOGRAPHY OF THE NON-INSTITUTIONAL CHURCHES OF CHRIST

Without a doubt, the most important volume on the history of the non-institutional Churches of Christ is David Edwin Harrell Jr.'s *The Churches of Christ in the Twentieth Century: Homer Hailey's Personal Journey of Faith*. Harrell's *magnum opus* contains both a biographical treatment of Hailey and a broader historical examination of Churches of Christ writ large. "Homer Hailey's life," he contends, "weaves its way through the twentieth-century history of churches of Christ in a way that illuminates the entire history of the movement."[36] The institutional division of the mid-twentieth century features prominently in Harrell's work, as do subsequent divisions within the smaller fellowship of non-institutional churches—including the controversy over Hailey's teachings on divorce and remarriage, a debate in which Harrell himself was a participant.

Harrell's influence as a scholar (and member) of non-institutional Churches of Christ also extended into his role as an advisor of doctoral students in the history department at Auburn University. Former Harrell student John C. Hardin's dissertation and contribution to a Harrell festschrift both examine the institutional division using the career of mainstream Churches of Christ figure Benton Cordell Goodpasture as a framing device. Goodpasture, who served as editor of the widely-read *Gospel Advocate* newspaper, spearheaded an effort to "quarantine" preachers holding non-institutional beliefs from the larger body of the fellowship. While Hardin's work does not challenge Harrell's interpretation of the division as a whole, it does usefully provide a counterpoint to it by exploring the controversy over the shoulder of a figure from the other side of the institutional split.[37]

Aside from Harrell, the most notable historian working within the non-institutional Churches of Christ is likely Steve Wolfgang. Much of Wolfgang's scholarship has focused on other issues related to the history of Churches of Christ; his master's thesis explored the connections between the fellowship and Fundamentalism, for instance, and his dissertation focused on the interplay of religion and science within the Restoration Movement.[38] But the historian and minister has also offered an account of the institutional division in which he argues that World War II accelerated doctrinal and practical changes already taking place within the mainstream Churches of Christ. These congregations, Wolfgang contends, came to believe that their new schools and missionary organizations were essential to the work of the church, and "it was an easy step to elevate their value well above whatever questionable virtue the maintenance of fellowship with the cantankerous 'antis' might possess. Noninstitutional brethren could be deemed expendable if they could not agree to go along and get along."[39]

Two additional sources from members of non-institutional Churches of Christ add usefully to our knowledge of the fellowship. Though more of a celebration of the school than a traditional work of scholarship, *Making a Difference: Florida College: The First Fifty Years* (edited by Margie H. Garrett) serves as a key record about the only center of higher education with close ties to the non-institutional Churches of Christ. The book, richly ornamented with photos of the campus and notable figures from its history, contains a number of essays from faculty members, alumni, and others connected to the school; collectively, these contributions detail Florida College's struggles and successes during its first half-century of existence.[40] Another important compendium of information on the non-institutional wing is a widely circulated outline of Ferrell Jenkins's presentation from the 1998 Pepperdine University Bible Lectures, titled "Please Don't Call Us 'Anti.'" While offering a historical overview of the movement is not Jenkins's primary concern, his talk does provide a useful snapshot of the state of the group in the late 1990s, as well as an accounting of the scholarship on the non-institutional congregations which existed at the time.[41]

Additionally, a handful of articles on smaller, similarly-minded fellowships of Churches of Christ provide useful points of comparison with the non-institutional wing, even though they are not themselves part of it. Larry Hart, Kent Ellett, and Thomas A. Langford have all offered treatments of the non-Sunday-School Churches of Christ, so called because of their members' belief that Sunday School classes constitute an unscriptural addition to the work of the church.[42] Similarly, Ron Clark has traced the history of the Mutual Edification churches, whose name derives from their conviction that "each congregation mutually edified or encouraged its members without the aid of a located or paid minister."[43] To be sure, the differences between these smaller groups and the non-institutional churches should not be elided. Nevertheless, the principled objections raised by such groups to various practices within mainstream churches often strongly resemble those voiced by their non-institutional brethren, even if they differ as to the propriety of the specific issue or issues under consideration.

HISTORIOGRAPHY OF THE INTERNATIONAL CHURCHES OF CHRIST

Only two scholarly monographs—one in sociology, the other in history—have focused exclusively on the International Churches of Christ. The first of these is Kathleen E. Jenkins's 2005 study, *Awesome Families: The Promise of Healing Relationships in the International Churches of Christ.* Building on an earlier journal article which covered racial and cultural diversity within the ICOC,[44] Jenkins contends that the church's rapid growth in the 1990s stemmed from its "therapeutic promise to heal, fortify, and construct" strong families and marriages.[45] As a sociologist, Jenkins rests her case primarily on fieldwork, which involved studying a single congregation in great depth over a period of several years. However, she supplements this research by delving into a number of ICOC texts and visual sources and by tracking movement-wide developments online, particularly during the tumultuous years of 2003 and 2004.[46] Jenkins does not give much attention to the history of the ICOC in *Awesome Families*, though she does devote a few pages to the movement's "creation story," outlined most influentially by founder Kip McKean. This story, according to Jenkins, was "a myth of unmatched evangelical growth, [and] was in the forefront of group discourse."[47] Jenkins also gives a brief outline of McKean's later removal from power and his subsequent attempts to reestablish control over the movement from Portland, Oregon.[48]

The other key scholarly monograph on the ICOC, also published in 2005, is C. Foster Stanback's *Into All Nations: A History of the International Churches of Christ*. Stanback's book, a richly detailed denominational history, traces the ICOC from its inception in 1979 through the upheavals of the early 2000s. Stanback, a member of the ICOC, argues that the group "has gradually moved toward greater institutionalization, a process that has rapidly accelerated following McKean's transition to a less prominent role in the leadership of the church."[49] Like Jenkins, Stanback writes from the chaos of the early-to-middle 2000s, and he shares her concern that McKean's maneuverings would lead to a major division within (if not necessarily the outright collapse of) the ICOC in coming years.[50] Yet he takes great care to situate the ICOC within its longer historical context as well, linking it back to the discipling movement of Chuck Lucas and even earlier efforts at campus ministry within mainstream Churches of Christ.

Into All Nations dovetails nicely with another work published two years later, Thomas A. Jones's memoir *In Search of a City: An Autobiographical Perspective on a Remarkable but Controversial Movement*. Though not an academic history of the ICOC, Jones's status as someone "connected almost continuously with this movement from its earliest days to the present day" allows him to speak to many of the same events as Stanback, yet from a participant's perspective.

Jones's work in particular serves as a useful historiographical corrective regarding ICOC leader Kip McKean; while Jones does not shy away from describing the circumstances which led to McKean's removal, he also acknowledges that "in all my interactions with him I never remember a time when I was not treated with respect."[51] Such passages offer a more nuanced version of McKean than is found in many works on the ICOC, a view which is neither totally affectionate nor entirely alarmist.

A handful of other writers have undertaken histories of the ICOC or its antecedent groups, often focusing on some particular aspect of the movement's past. One of the earliest is Don Vinzant's 1988 essay which describes five theological influences on the discipling movement that later give rise to the ICOC. Vinzant's is not a charitable evaluation, and he seeks to distance Churches of Christ from the discipling trend:

> The fact that it has been tried by others is rather embarrassing to those who thought that someone in the churches of Christ invented this approach. The reality, however, is that churches of Christ are among the last ones to be damaged by the discipling movement.[52]

In subsequent years, Russell R. Paden sought to illuminate the historical connections between the ICOC and the mainstream Churches of Christ, pushing back on Vinzant's thesis that the groups were almost totally separate. "The conclusion of this study is that the groups are closer in attitude and doctrine than either cares to acknowledge," Paden writes in his master's thesis, and "while the Boston Movement has introduced some practices that are foreign to and have origins outside the Churches of Christ, both bodies remain quite similar in doctrine and attitude."[53] Paden continued developing these thoughts in contributions to two edited collections, Timothy Miller's *America's Alternative Religions* and Michael W. Casey and Douglas A. Foster's *The Stone-Campbell Movement: An International Religious Tradition*.[54] Similarly, Roger D. Hendricks and John F. Wilson have offered interpretations which support Paden's position that the ICOC owes much to mainstream Churches of Christ, even as it differs from them in a number of respects.[55]

HISTORIOGRAPHY OF THE EMERGING CHURCH MOVEMENT

Like the International Churches of Christ, the Emerging Church Movement is such a recent phenomenon that there has been little time for historical scholarship on the group to develop; though a great deal of academic attention has been devoted to the ECM, it has more often been in the disciplines of sociology and theology. Nevertheless, a handful of historians and other scholars of religion have sketched out the general contours of ECM history, and their divergent interpretations allow us to explore briefly how the story of the ECM has changed over time.

In 2014, Gerardo Marti and Gladys Ganiel included a brief examination of ECM history in their masterful sociological study *The Deconstructed Church: Understanding Emerging Christianity*. Although precursors of the movement can be found as far back as the late 1970s, they write, the direct antecedents of the ECM in the United States originated with missions and youth ministry revitalization efforts two decades later. Like several other observers, including Mark Driscoll, they argue for the central importance of the Young Leaders Network and its parent organization Leadership Network to the eventual development of the ECM.[56] Yet Marti and Ganiel also caution against historical interpretations which see the ECM as solely an offshoot of evangelicalism. Instead, they argue that while "evangelicalism is the seed" which contained the ECM, "the ecumenical movement has, almost unnoticed, provided the fertile soil in which it has grown."[57]

That same year, American religious historian Steven P. Miller devoted a couple of pages in *The Age of Evangelicalism: America's Born-Again Years* to the ECM, defining the group as "an energetic, if somewhat amorphous, community of young evangelicals who sought to break away from the modern evangelical establishment." Miller notes the enormous influence of pastor and author Brian McLaren on the movement, as well as its prioritization of missional living and adoption of the language of postmodernism. But he also concludes that while breaking away from the evangelical establishment has been a core goal for many ECM members, "the language of departure was a bit misleading" because the ECM still strongly resembles "part of a revived evangelical left."[58]

The lengthiest historical overview of the ECM to date, name of said overview notwithstanding, is Michael Clawson's "A Brief History of the Emerging Church Movement in the United States." In this contribution to a multidisciplinary edited collection, Clawson notes the relative dearth of historical scholarship on the ECM, as well as the irony that "a movement so dependent on historical claims for its very raison d'être" has engendered so little historical inquiry. He provides the most sophisticated and thorough accounting of ECM origins to date, identifying three primary theological and methodological streams flowing into the movement: 1) the methodologically experimental 'new paradigm' churches of the late-twentieth century emerging out of the evangelical youth sub-culture, the Jesus People Movement, and Church Growth methodologies during the 1960s and 70s; 2) the missional theology developing out of the works of Leslie Newbigin and David Bosch; and 3) the movement of socially and politically progressive evangelicals produced by the political upheavals of the 1960s and informed by integral mission theology coming out of Latin America.[59]

Clawson's identification of these geographically diverse influences is bolstered by the work of Mathew Guest, whose 2017 article "The Emerging Church in Transatlantic Perspective" goes a step further by showing how local conditions, including predominant religious cultures and reigning denominational configurations, have impacted ECM identity formation in different parts of the world.[60]

A ROADMAP FROM REVELATION TO RECURSION

In the first chapter, "Revelation," we will examine how restorationist Christians' beliefs about the nature of Scripture—the primary means of accessing the life and times of the first century church—have changed across generations and varied between groups. The following chapter, "Recalibration," illustrates that the normative era of the "early church" is itself subject to some variation; while most primitivist Christians have limited themselves to restoring the church as described in the New Testament, others have felt at liberty to draw on other sources from, and even other generations of, the Christian past. (This chapter focuses exclusively on the Emerging Church Movement and briefly overviews its institutional history at the outset.) "Replication," the subsequent chapter, focuses on how members of the different groups have answered a crucial, if sometimes unrecognized, question: can the church of the first century truly be mirrored in another, or are there aspects of early church life which are beyond the reach of modern believers? The final chapter, "Recursion," reveals what happens when restorationists unconsciously begin seeking to recover their own movement's origins along with those of the early church. "Repetition," a short epilogue, briefly summarizes the conclusions of the preceding chapters and gestures toward areas of potentially productive research.

First, though, "Revelation." Most restorationist Christians have, in some form or fashion, affirmed their trust in the accuracy and authority of Christian scripture. The Bible offers guidance for an individual believer seeking to live a worthy life, they agree, but also a set of blueprints for the restoration of the long-lost early church. Yet this confidence can be undercut by two questions that restorationist groups have had to answer, whether knowingly or unknowingly: does the Bible require interpretation, and if so, what roles might higher education and biblical scholarship have in that endeavor? Scottish Common Sense Realism, a philosophical school which has provided many of the Stone-Campbell Movement's hermeneutical underpinnings, looms large in each of the groups' responses to these concerns.

1

REVELATION

For readers of the New Testament, the word "revelation" may, somewhat paradoxically, connote confusion rather than clarity. "Many people today regard Revelation as the hardest" of the Christian scriptures, theologian N.T. Wright has observed, in no small measure due to its "strange, lurid and sometimes bizarre and violent imagery."[1] This paradoxical sense of interpretive unease regarding one specific revelation stands in stark contrast to the term's usage in most other contexts, where it generally refers to the acquisition of understanding, often of divine provenance—for instance, the assertion of scholar of law and literature Mitchell Meltzer that "a revelation is what we would not know by secular means alone."[2]

Revelation can be found in silence, too. Philosopher Peter Alward has argued that "narrative informants—[the] non-actual fact tellers... whom storytellers pretend to be"—reveal information to their audiences not only by what they say directly but also via the "propositions which they do not assert...."[3] Benedek Láng has made a compelling case that the ciphers used in late medieval magical texts, which might at first glance seem to be "tools for hiding the message," were instead meant "to call attention to the ritual of the text... Their mysterious appearance worked more like a strategy of exposure, an advertisement by means of the rhetoric of secrecy."[4] And speaking of magic, Michael Taussig has perceptively noted that "The real skill of the practitioner lies not in skilled concealment but in the skilled revelation of skilled concealment. Magic is efficacious not despite the trick but on account of its exposure."[5] Again, to emphasize the point, "revelation" is usually thought to bring its recipients clarity and insight, not confusion and insecurity, regardless of the specific form that the revelation itself takes.

Whatever difficulties may inhere within the interpretation of John's capital-R Revelation, restorationists have typically evinced a high degree of trust in the reliability and accessibility of God's lowercase-r revelation, broadly speaking. These Christians' beliefs about the Bible and the way(s) in which its truths are revealed to believers form one core aspect of their historical ecclesiologies, or conceptions about the early church. The Bible is not only a source of moral guidance for these believers but a vessel for accurate and trustworthy blueprints which reveal both the style and substance of early Christianity. These convictions help frame restorationists' historical ecclesiologies by establishing the bounds of what is accepted as the authentic, divinely proffered history of the church to be restored.

Despite the trust that many restorationists have placed in the reliability of Scripture's revelations, issues about the interpretation of those revelations by human audiences have proven more difficult to resolve. Restorationists, either directly or indirectly, have had to deal with two closely related questions regarding their interpretation of divine revelation. First, is biblical truth self-evident to the honest seeker, or does Scripture necessarily require some sort of effort beyond mere surface reading on the reader's part? And second, if the Bible does have to be interpreted somehow, what roles (if any) do higher education and biblical scholarship play in that process?[6] The ways in which Christadelphians, non-institutional Churches of Christ, and International Churches of Christ in particular have answered these questions have been powerfully shaped by an underlying, though often unconscious, commitment to the tenets of Scottish Common Sense Realism. As such, it is to a brief overview of that philosophical school's influence on the larger Stone-Campbell Movement that we must first turn before we explore how those three groups have engaged with higher education and biblical scholarship as part of their restoration projects.[7]

(HOW) DO WE INTERPRET THE BIBLE?

Speaking in general terms about the arch-Common Sensers' impact on American religion, Sydney E. Ahlstrom observed that "few, if any, philosophers have had to suffer such ignominious re-evaluations as Thomas Reid and Dugald Stewart," but also that the repeated, vigorous challenges to their ideas demonstrate just how thoroughly "Scottish Realism penetrated American thought."[8] To that end, D.F Kelly, writing in the *Evangelical Dictionary of Theology*, notes that

"Scottish philosophy... provided the epistemological structure utilized by both 'liberals' and 'conservatives' in nineteenth-century America."[9] Additionally, Catholic theologian and historian Luigi Giussani has noted the impact of "Scottish Realism and Reid's common sense" on the writings of Charles Hodge, whose theological works, which served as standard reading in Calvinist Presbyterian circles, "stressed the doctrinal aspects that were then analyzed and upheld with scholastic rigor."[10]

What were the chief tenets of common sense, though? James Fieser contends that each of the school's major philosophers responded in some way to David Hume's "sceptical assault on the adequacy of human reason... by appealing to instinctive common sense principles." While some opted for terms with fewer built-in implications than the titular "common sense"—terms such as "first truths" and "primary principles" often served as stand-ins—they nevertheless agreed that humans innately share certain foundational true beliefs about the world and the way it works.[11] S.A. Grave concurs that the philosophy "arose as an 'answer' to Hume" and specifically to his skepticism that the senses accurately relayed the existence of an external world.[12] Scottish Common Sense Realism proponents, in contrast to Hume, held that the reality of that external world was no less likely than any competing skeptical hypothesis (Descartes's evil demon, for instance) and that it had the added benefits of conforming to both common sense and human experience.[13] The common sense philosophy was not entirely a reaction to Hume, however; Peter Novick acknowledges the SCSR philosophers' immense intellectual debt to Francis Bacon—or at least "a simplified and considerably vulgarized version of his views"—in their prioritization of "a rigidly empirical approach" and "the scrupulous avoidance of hypotheses, scorned by Bacon as 'phantoms.'"[14]

The application of this common sense philosophy, with its promises of certainty and accessibility, to the study of Scripture has powerfully shaped the inductive hermeneutics used within Stone-Campbell Movement circles.[15] Carisse Mickey Berryhill explains further that the approach formed "the expectation that everyone could and should know the Bible" because its truths were freely accessible and available to all.[16] Though few within Stone-Campbell Movement circles today would be prone to appeal directly to the writings of Reid, Stewart, and company to prove a point, the men's philosophy has continued to guide hermeneutical approaches from behind the scenes. David H. Warren has narrated how both Thomas Campbell and Alexander Campbell came into contact with the common-sense ideals that served as "the basic elements for change" in their movement.[17] Moving forward in time, Richard T. Hughes notes that David Lipscomb, a Nashville minister and leading movement figure throughout the second half of the nineteenth century, "routinely employed the Baconian common sense method of Bible interpretation... [but] spent little time discussing either the method as such or Francis Bacon, its alleged founder."[18] Similarly, David Edwin Harrell Jr., speaking of the late nineteenth/early twentieth century division between Disciples of Christ and Churches of Christ, argues that those in the second group "were united by a commonsense hermeneutic that believed that the New Testament provided a recoverable model of Christianity, though they were far from united about the details of the model."[19] Even John C. Nugent, who has argued that "Alexander Campbell's reform was driven *primarily* by eschatological and ecumenical concerns," rather than Scottish Common Sense Realism, acknowledges that Campbell "was shaped by the philosophical categories of his day... [even as] he also transformed them and subordinated them to his more fundamental ecclesial concerns."[20]

Hughes's previously quoted description of David Lipscomb could just as easily and just as accurately be applied to many of the historical subjects of this work. Although these later restorationists rarely, if ever, discussed common sense philosophy or namechecked Reid or Stewart directly, Scottish Common Sense Realism nevertheless provided the philosophical underpinnings for many within Christadelphianism, the non-institutional Churches of Christ, and the International Churches of Christ well into the twentieth and even twenty-first centuries. The continued influence of the common sense philosophy can be seen in those group members' tentative, hesitant, and uncertain embraces of biblical scholarship, and higher education more broadly, in the pursuit of an accurate conception of the early church.

CHRISTADELPHIAN COMMON SENSE

Members of Christadelphian predecessor groups, such as the Royal Association of Believers, often evinced a strong skepticism toward formal theological education, viewing it as little more than a stepping stone toward heretical, anti-restorationist beliefs rooted in human (mis)understanding rather than in divine revelation. During and after their fallout over rebaptism for converts from other Christian traditions, the Christadelphian founder John Thomas took Alexander Campbell to task for, in Thomas's estimation, backtracking on his earlier opposition to seminary training for ministers. One example of this harsh criticism of Campbell and his Bethany College can be found in the first volume of Thomas's *Herald of the Kingdom and Age to Come*:

> This is the Theological Seminary of the New Sect, known in these States as 'the Campbellites.' Its founder and president is the Rev. Alexander Campbell after whom the denomination is named. In the early part of his career he was inveterately opposed to schools for the education of young men for the ministry; but by the following extract from his Millennial Harbinger, it appears he now approves them, and is greatly in favor of *Alma Matres* and endowments![21]

Again, Thomas's lambasting of Campbell stemmed from his belief that his opponent, once a strident critic of the trappings of other Christian denominations, had backslid into both the structures ("*Alma Matres* and endowments") and language ("Theological Seminary," "the Rev. Alexander Campbell") of those impure churches. According to Thomas, given the lack of biblical warrant for these aberrations from the example of the earliest Christians, Campbell's restorationism was dangerously incomplete and insufficiently distinguishable from the moribund faith of wider Christendom. Thomas would also criticize Campbell's school at a later date for, in his estimation, unduly minimizing the authority and intelligence of the apostles, whose teachings and practices laid the groundwork for believers not only in the first century but in the nineteenth as well. In the tellingly named "Apostolic Foolishness Better than College Wisdom," Thomas claimed that "historians of Christ's church, professors of Sacred History, college students, and those that patronize them," including the guilty parties at Campbell's Bethany College, all missed the blindingly obvious truth which was apparent to the apostles: "that David's kingdom and throne will be assuredly restored to Israel as in the days of old[.]"[22]

Yet even though Thomas had little regard for theological education like that offered at Bethany, he was hardly an opponent of in-depth study of the Bible or of higher education in other disciplines. As to the former, Thomas's eschatological fascinations led him to focus much of his time and energy on the Book of Revelation, and in 1861, in the first volume of *Eureka: An Exposition of the Apocalypse in Harmony with "the Things of the Kingdom of the Deity and the Name of Jesus Anointed,"* he sought to unveil the one true interpretation of that difficult biblical text. Thomas argued that such knowledge had always remained hidden, but that diligent study had revealed to him the timing of the events leading to the advent:

> But though this remarkable prophecy has been so long extant, no scriptural, logical, and consistent exposition of it has any existence in the world. "The servants of the Deity," for whose information and use it was revealed, have, doubtless, understood its teaching....They could not, however, demonstrate its [sic] historically, of course, except as its predictions were gradually developed.[23]

Remarkably, Thomas argues that modern believers, through careful study and proper interpretation of the biblical texts, can actually understand more than those living in earlier generations could ever hope to achieve. He acknowledges that the earliest Christians did have a tentative grasp of the importance of the later sections of Revelation, in that they realized that those events had not yet come to pass. But, from their vantage point, they had no way to fully understand how the images described by John would play out over the course of history. According to Thomas, though, *Eureka* offered the first correct explanation of Revelation's opening chapters, which made possible "a correct explanation of the parts of this wonderful book which have become *historical*."[24] With that knowledge, believers in Thomas's day could accurately discern when Jesus would return—to see further ahead than the original believers could. Far from being self-evident, the truths of Revelation required diligent study to correctly interpret, but with effort, Thomas contended, they could be (and had been) unlocked.[25]

Nor was John Thomas himself an unlearned man. Religious historian Charles Lippy has helpfully reconstructed Thomas's early life in Britain, which included extensive training for and a promising career as a surgeon in and around London. Thomas studied medicine under several independent surgeons and at St. Thomas's Hospital, where he may also have helped teach human anatomy as a demonstrator. Additionally, he read and defended a paper in front of the London Medical Society and published a number of articles in *Lancet*, which was (and is) one of the top medical journals in the world.[26] Although Thomas would, in the long run, use his medical training as a means of supporting his ministry rather than as the groundwork for an academic career, it is clear that education was not in and of itself a stumbling block for Thomas.

Given John Thomas's deep personal involvement in in-depth Bible study and in higher education broadly construed, then, his attacks on Alexander Campbell and Bethany College are better understood as a manifestation of his larger restorationist vision rather than as a display of some sort of inherently anti-intellectual tendency. To be sure, his imbibing of the common sense philosophy led him to oppose seminaries and formal licensure for ministers as unbiblical additions to the example of the early Christians. Yet the philosophy did not, for Thomas, fully collapse the distance between the biblical texts and the reader—Revelation had to be studied and interpreted, after all—nor did it necessitate a broader array of anti-intellectual sympathies on his part. Later generations of Christadelphian believers, particularly those living in the twentieth and twenty-first centuries, have proven even more amenable than Thomas to the development of a distinctly Christadelphian scholarly apparatus, though that trend has not yet culminated in the creation of a Christadelphian university or seminary.

One important step toward this kind of deeper, at least semi-academic engagement with the Bible was taken by American Christadelphians in 1923 with the creation of the first Christadelphian "Bible school."[27] These inter-congregational assemblies, typically held annually, have taken "their educational and instructional raison d'etre seriously," according to Lippy. "A typical daily schedule might include a morning exhortation, three formal classes with separate groups for children and youth taught by women, and an evening exhortation"—and this demanding agenda might be repeated daily for one or even two weeks.[28] Additionally, Margaret Ann Ross has counterpoised the Christadelphian Bible School located in Faulkner County, Arkansas, with the camp meetings of other religious groups in the area. Writing in the *Arkansas Historical Quarterly* in 1951, Ross argued that unlike other pioneer camp meetings, the Christadelphian school had "no mourner's bench; no long sermons on repentance; no sawdust floors; [and] no shouting" but instead served as an institution run by "competent instructors" for Christadelphians "(1) To build each other up in our most holy faith and (2) To teach interested persons the way of life."[29]

Another major milestone in the history of Christadelphian engagement with biblical scholarship was the 2007 creation of the *Christadelphian eJournal of Biblical Interpretation*. Though not a typical academic journal—articles are subject to review by an editorial board rather than traditional peer review, for instance—the publication's founding editors explicitly sought to meet their fellowship's evident need for a "journal that covers *academic* biblical studies."

> Human beings are imperfect knowing creatures and there is much error in doctrine and practice in Christian churches; this extends to associated secular and confessional academic biblical study. On the other hand, within the Christadelphian community, there are errors in interpretation of scripture in our published materials and our ongoing thinking. However, it is a premise of this eJournal that the Christadelphian community has a

> deposit of doctrinal principles which aid the correct interpretation of scripture. These help filter out errors in secular and confessional academic bible study, but as Christadelphian interpretation comes into contact with such Bible study, there is a need for the *presentation* of that interpretation to change and thereby engage with the churches.[30]

As evidenced here, the editors clearly understood there to be room for both academic biblical scholarship and a distinctly Christadelphian interpretation of Scripture in the modern work of the Christadelphian movement. These things in no way undermined the correct understanding of biblical teachings in the present day but indeed were the things which made it possible: "churches need to 'turn' away from many traditions in practice and interpretation that they have accrued since the times of the early church fathers," the editors asserted, and "the purpose of this eJournal [is] to add to the Christadelphian witness for such a 'turning'."[31]

COMMON SENSE AND COMMON CENTS

The Christadelphians were not the only members of a small SCM fellowship to have to reconcile a longstanding commitment to a common sense hermeneutic with a perceived need for more intellectually rigorous engagement with Scripture. Equally indebted to the SCSR-influenced hermeneutic,[32] members of non-institutional Churches of Christ have, to an even greater degree than the Christadelphians, engaged with higher education and biblical scholarship on a sustained basis—though not without reservations of their own. In particular, the most important concern voiced by members of the non-institutional wing throughout the twentieth century was that church-sponsored schools stood to threaten the congregational autonomy and spiritual authority of elderships so prized by their movement—two key components of the ecclesial governance which they believed was not just preferable but a mandatory element of the restorationist blueprints.

One of the gravest threats which Christian institutions of higher learning posed to the biblical model of church governance, prominent non-institutional figures argued, was that the tendency of colleges and universities to expand in size and scope could lead them to infringe on the God-given authority of individual congregations and the elderships which led them. Writing about Central Christian College (a predecessor of the current Oklahoma Christian University) in the *Gospel Guardian* in 1951, G.K. Wallace praised the school "because it in no way tries to form a connection with the church." This restraint, Wallace continued, stemmed from the strong leadership of President L.R. Wilson and those working for him, who all "know the difference between the church and a school." For Wallace and others, there was a clear distinction between the divine directives given to the church in the New Testament and the potentially helpful, though perhaps not essential, work of Christian colleges. "Let the church do the work of the church," he pleaded, and "let the school do the work of the school."[33]

John T. Lewis had raised similar concerns in the *Bible Banner*, a predecessor paper to the *Gospel Guardian*, a little over a decade earlier. Lewis perceptively noted the influence, positive or negative, that Christian higher education could and would have on the movement as a whole. "There is no doubt that for the next few decades the way 'our' Bible colleges go the Churches will go," he wrote, "and herein is the danger." In particular, Lewis worried about where university administrators' ultimate allegiance and accountability would rest when push came to shove. Would they hold true to their religious convictions regardless of what donors or accreditors had to say, he wondered, or would outside forces bring enough pressure to bear to substantially impact the nature of the education the schools provided?

> Let no one think that I am an enemy of any of our colleges. I am not; but I am fearful of the ultimate end of the course they have chartered - Endowments, that will attract human vultures, and standardize accreditations, dictated by men who would not give a whoop whether the teachers were modernists, agnostics, infidels, or what not; but could whoop it up, if you got one of their tribe and wanted to fire him, or tell him what he could not teach.[34]

As with John Thomas of the Christadelphians, Lewis's remarks must be read in the context of his own life experiences, which included education at the Nashville Bible School, a forerunner of the modern Lipscomb University.[35] Still, his worries would be echoed by others in the non-institutional congregations, and those members who sought to undertake educational ventures would take great care to ward off even the perception that the proper relationship between church and school had in some way been compromised. For instance, G.K. Wallace, in the article on Central Christian College cited above, also called on churches to not overstep the bounds of their scope and authority in support of the colleges, either: "If it is the work of the church let the church do it; if it is not the work of the church let the church stay out of it."[36]

Concerns about church governance and fears of schools encroaching on ecclesial authority, however, did not categorically prevent members of non-institutional Churches of Christ from viewing Christian higher education positively or from giving their allegiance to the one school associated with their wing of the movement, Florida College.[37] James R. (Jim) Cope, who became FC's president in 1949, articulated in the *Gospel Guardian* the following year a vision of Christian education which placed the study of the Bible front and center: "It was the idea of giving young people Bible teaching in connection with their secular studies that prompted the founding of all our Christian schools." Those studies in other disciplines were important, too, of course, and Cope claimed that whatever "Florida Christian College does in these lines it proposes to be of the highest quality. The Word of God, however, is the center of the entire curriculum and we have neither desire nor inclination to make it otherwise."[38]

Nor was there any desire, according to Colly Caldwell, who later served as president of the school, to intertwine the school with Churches of Christ in any official capacity. "Foremost [of the school's founding principles] was a basic conviction that the school should be kept organically independent of churches." This guideline did, of course, have to be reconciled with the directive that "all members of the governing board of directors, all administrators, and all faculty members be faithful members of local churches of

Christ." The goal, though, was to create "an environment consistent with faith in Christ" without doing "the work of churches" or trying "to influence the actions of churches."[39]

To that end, Florida College would adopt a different attitude toward funding—specifically, toward accepting contributions from congregations of Churches of Christ—than the other schools associated with Churches of Christ writ large. Though in its earliest years, during the presidency of L.R. Wilson, the college accepted (but did not ask for) donations from congregations, the Board of Trustees announced soon after his resignation that it would no longer accept even these unsolicited donations. "The shift from nonsolicitation to nonacceptance of church contributions," historian and non-institutional member Ed Harrell has argued, "positioned [Florida College] squarely in the camp of the noninstitutional churches of Christ."[40] In fact, Cope's convictions on this matter played at least some role in his selection as the school's second president. According to Clinton D. Hamilton, Cope had been "studying in detail" whether congregations could cooperate in funding a Christian college, and "he could find no scriptures that authorized churches to support... independent colleges wherein the Bible was taught."[41] Again, this is not to say that Cope, or anyone else involved, felt that Christian higher education was pointless or even harmful—he did accept the presidency of the school, after all. But while FC could and should play a role in establishing a Christian environment in which students could grow spiritually and in their knowledge of the Bible, a common-sense reading of the New Testament, in Cope's view, precluded congregations from cooperating in that regard because of a lack of scriptural warrant.

COMMON SENSE IN THE INTERNATIONAL CHURCHES OF CHRIST—AND BEYOND

The common sense philosophy has likewise played a key role in shaping the theology of the International Churches of Christ, the youngest of the three groups featured in this chapter, despite the significant stylistic differences between the ICOC and the older Christadelphian and non-institutional wings. One unlikely example of this lasting influence was the March 26, 1995, issue of *L.A. Story*, the flagship publication of the ICOC during that decade. Numerous color photographs, magazine-quality layout and design, and a front cover stylized to look like a movie poster all combined to make a powerful statement to the reader: the Los Angeles Church of Christ was a modern church, totally aware of and fully connected to its unusually glamorous surroundings. This particular issue of the bulletin was devoted to the congregation's fifth annual Women's Day event, which had just been held in conjunction with similar programs at other congregations throughout the ICOC. "Women of every race, color, age and background imaginable" combined to form "what was probably the largest gathering of women in God's modern-day movement," according to Gloria Baird, one of the event's organizers. And although the weather was uncharacteristically overcast for the location, the event was a success, with over 3,600 visitors joining the roughly 2,400 women of the church for the program.[42] Related articles on the following pages delved into other aspects of the event's past and present; for instance, one recounted how a previous year's Women's Day had led to the conversion of "a cool artist living the fast party life" and described how one of her "old night club haunts" had itself been converted to "a place where Christians gather to worship God, appropriately renamed 'The UPSIDE DOWN Club.'"[43]

Yet for all of the glitz and glam of the bulletin itself, the women who contributed articles to the issue espoused a rather traditional view of Scripture, reflecting their fellowship's Stone-Campbell Movement heritage.[44] Megan Blackwell, who spoke at the L.A. event, was quoted as having said that "we want to pick the Bible apart, but in actuality, the Bible picks us apart."[45] Gloria Baird compared other prominent women in the ICOC to "modern-day Esthers and Deborahs" and stated that one of the greatest impacts of the Women's Day was that "hundreds of women are now studying the Bible to become disciples."[46] Most notably, Elena Garcia-McKean, wife of ICOC founder Kip McKean, wrote that the Bible provided "timeless wisdom for life, even in the 90's," and asserted that the event was an answer to her years of prayer for a gathering "where the glory and power of God would radiate from women teaching the Bible."[47] While none of these contributors engaged in any systematic discussion about the nature of Scripture, such references nevertheless revealed an underlying belief that the Bible was the source of unchanging examples for the modern church and a sure guide for disciples on the path to salvation.

This conviction should come as little surprise to those familiar with the ICOC's ancestry. With its roots firmly planted in the Churches of Christ and the broader Stone-Campbell Movement, the ICOC historical ecclesiology has continued to reflect many of the same common sense principles and assumptions as those of its forebears. And like the Christadelphians and members of the non-institutional

Churches of Christ, ICOC members have increasingly embraced biblical scholarship and higher education, even while expressing some skepticism or doubt about those endeavors.

To wit, several leading figures within the International Churches of Christ, and its predecessor Crossroads and Boston Movements, were the products of theological or seminary training. (Others earned advanced degrees in different disciplines—for instance, Al Baird, who held a PhD in physics and published several articles in the field prior to his work with the church.)[48] While a number of theses and dissertations on the ICOC were completed by non-members during the 1990s, some quite skeptical or negative in tone,[49] the graduate work undertaken by church leaders during that same decade testifies to the importance many of them placed on graduate-level theological education.

Although the DMin projects completed by ICOC leaders could be engaged with by scholars as secondary sources in other venues, for our purposes, their mere existence is primary evidence of an underlying ICOC commitment to graduate level training in theological disciplines. This commitment, in fact, predates the church's adoption of the ICOC name. A leading figure throughout much of the church's early history, Marty Wooten completed a DMin at the Harding Graduate School of Religion in 1990; in his thesis, he argued that the Boston Church served as a "revitalization movement" within Churches of Christ as a whole. Two other ICOC notables, Douglas Jacoby and Steve Kinnard, each completed DMins at Drew University in 1999. Jacoby thanks several prominent ICOC members, including the McKeans and Bairds, in the acknowledgements to his project, while Kinnard writes that the chief purpose of his project was to "develop multimedia tools from a center in Jerusalem to educate members throughout the International Church of Christ."[50] Again, the academic and ministerial value of these projects is outside our scope of consideration here, but the simple reality that these three leaders sought out and completed doctoral programs illustrates that formal theological or ministerial training was seen as beneficial by at least some among the church's top brass.

Having said this, it is important to acknowledge that the theological education of a Wooten, Jacoby, or Kinnard was not always the norm. In his 2014 master's thesis, ICOC minister James Lappeman argues that the overwhelming church-wide emphasis on evangelism from the late 1970s through the early 2000s meant that "success in converting people" rather than formal training became "the dominant mark of a trained and faithful minister."[51] This prioritizing of a results-oriented leadership paradigm, Lappeman notes, was slowed somewhat by the presence of former members of Churches of Christ in the upper echelons of the ICOC hierarchy in the early years. "While the core Boston Movement leadership came from a CoC background, with at least some formal theological education," Lappeman argues, "the balance began to shift" as the ICOC ranks swelled with converts from other backgrounds during the 1980s and 1990s.[52]

Furthermore, Lappeman conducted interviews with several prominent ICOC leaders from the 1990s, including Baird, Jacoby, and Kinnard. Baird, according to Lappeman, "described the mentorship training as a reaction to the overly academic practice in the CoC," an understanding articulated by others, including Gordon Ferguson (also interviewed by Lappeman), at least as far back as the late 1980s.[53] Jacoby, for his part, told the interviewer of multiple instances in which ICOC ministers were encouraged to pack up and travel to plant new churches instead of finishing their coursework, and both he and Kinnard claimed that none of the church's top-level "World Sector Leaders" had graduate-level theological degrees.[54]

Lappeman argues convincingly that while the ICOC's use of mentorship as its primary training method can be traced back to the antecedent Crossroads Movement and the leadership of Chuck Lucas, Kip McKean's complex views on formal theological education played an even larger role in shaping the church's relationship to biblical scholarship and higher education. McKean's antipathy, or at least ambivalence, is still evident today in his work with the SoldOut Discipling Movement, which broke away from the ICOC in the mid-2000s. Like many of the other early ICOC notables, McKean, the founder of that group, was a college graduate himself, having completed his undergraduate studies at the University of Florida in 1975.[55] Originally converting to Churches of Christ while living in Gainesville, McKean participated in Chuck Lucas's campus ministry at the Crossroads congregation and would later study at both Eastern Baptist Theological Seminary and the Harding Graduate School of Religion while working as a campus minister.[56]

A later account of McKean's life and ministry would claim, however, that McKean was not entirely satisfied with the training provided at schools like HGSR (now Harding School of Theology) which were affiliated with Churches of Christ:

> He concluded that though helpful in scholastic pursuits, a formal seminary – where future ministers' days were consumed with their academics and so were 'removed' from being immersed in the lives of people – was not the way to train evangelists. Rather, it is one minster [sic] walking with another like Jesus with His Twelve or Paul training Timothy and Titus. Yet, Kip especially appreciated his courses in church history and in the Old Testament, and so began to dream of a way to have day-to-day training in ministry combined with Bible courses.[57]

Despite McKean's stated ambivalence towards much of the Churches of Christ educational "system," he was, according to that same biography, also "influenced by former missionaries and the mission efforts especially by the Sunset School of Preaching – a Mainline Church of Christ school that trained preachers – located in Lubbock, Texas."[58]

Given the combination of McKean's seeming preference for mentorship-based training with his somewhat begrudging acknowledgement of the role that formal coursework played in his own development as a church leader, it is perhaps not too surprising that in 2012-2013, the SoldOut Discipling Movement launched its own International College of Christian Ministries in Los Angeles, California. "Every major 'Christian denomination' in the world has established their own seminary to formalize their doctrines and to train their ministers," according to McKean's biography, and the ICCM would serve those functions for the SoldOut Discipling Movement going forward by supplementing "Jesus' plan to train ministers by walking with them" with "more classroom oriented Biblical studies."[59] While the independence of the school from the church is open to question—one of its first actions was to grant various degrees to 94 church members on the basis of their life experiences as Evangelists and Women's Ministry Leaders, including a doctorate for McKean so that he could then serve as the first president of the school in a bit of chicken-or-egg maneuvering—the institution nevertheless reflects the culmination of a longstanding desire of McKean's.[60] Several dissertations and other projects completed by students at the school have since been published by SoldOut Press International, the church's in-house publishing arm; these include titles such as Elena McKean's *Elevate: Jesus' Global Revolution for Women*.[61]

CONCLUSION

Though the ideas of Reid, Stewart, and the other architects of Scottish Common Sense Realism carry less weight today than they once did among philosophers, the lasting influence of their worldview is nevertheless evident in the theological histories of the "Big Three" Stone-Campbell Movement fellowships and in those of the Christadelphians, non-institutional Churches of Christ, and International Churches of Christ. As we have seen already and will explore in greater depth in a later chapter on "replication," each of our three groups has historically been committed to the belief that the New Testament contains a clearly defined pattern for the church, which believers can and should restore in their own time. Yet as we have observed in this chapter, all three groups have also chosen to meaningfully engage with higher education and biblical studies, challenging the tendency of the common sense philosophy to remove the distance between the reader and the text by minimizing or denying outright the necessity of interpretation. The ways in which these fellowships have interacted with the divine revelation contained in the New Testament, again, comprise a foundational element of their historical ecclesiologies, in that that revelation is the raw material from which their conceptions of the early church are formed.

The following chapter, focusing exclusively on the Emerging Church Movement, will explore a second aspect of historical ecclesiology which I am calling "recalibration." Despite the broad agreements among restorationists that the distant Christian past provides some sort of exemplary model for later generations of believers to restore, and that the New Testament provides the blueprints for that restoration project, the exact chronological definition of the normative "early church" is still subject to some measure of debate. In the case of the ECM, terms like "ancient-future faith" or "vintage faith" bear more than a passing resemblance to the phrases, such as "first century church" or "early church" or "New Testament church," used in many restorationist circles. Yet the chronological parameters of the first two terms are significantly more expansive, often including several hundred years' worth of Christian history beyond what is covered in the New Testament. Does this kind of temporal flexibility categorically exclude the ECM from being properly considered "restorationist"? Perhaps a more flexible definition of "restorationist," which takes into account this recalibration of the normative church, is in order.

2

RECALIBRATION

Although the word "recalibration" might initially conjure up visions of white-coated scientists carefully fiddling with knobs on delicate and expensive equipment in a lab, in truth, the ongoing adjustment of the underlying settings and baseline assumptions of an idea is a common endeavor. Law professor Stuart Chinn, for example, has argued that the gradual recalibration of reform sentiments as they encounter norms and institutions in society is a necessary step in any instance of legal change. Rather than viewing this kind of collision as an unfortunate barrier to be overcome or avoided, Chinn instead contends that this interaction is the very thing "that endows vague and still-indeterminate reform principles with *operational meaning*. Recalibration processes do nothing less than define the substance of the initial reforms themselves."[1] From another perspective, the ongoing recalibration of risk perception also plays a major role in how countries evaluate, manage, and respond to the constantly shifting world of international relations. In this vein, as seen in Ra Mason's work, recalibration not only takes into account the "level of perceived risks" but also "how risks are conceptualized into forms which pose different kinds of potential harms and opportunities"—in other words, foreign policy recalibration must account for not only changes in the quantitative impact of possible outcomes, but also in the qualitative nature of the risk itself.[2] And as a recent working paper has shown, recalibrating the forecast probability distributions of long-range weather models based on the past performance of those models may lead to better predictions, even though a "forecast, being an expression of uncertainty about the future, is necessarily a probabilistic affair."[3]

The concept of recalibration is also germane to our discussion of historical ecclesiology and of restorationism more broadly conceived. Generally speaking, of course, restorationist Christians view the beliefs, practices, and other aspects of the lives of the first followers of Jesus as normative in some fashion—hence the rough synonym "primitivist."[4] Disciples of Christ historian and theologian Alfred T. DeGroot has gone even further, making the case that "the history of all continuing religions," not just Christianity, "is a record of recurring restoration programs." Each faith tradition in its own way and in its own time must seek renewal "by means of refreshment at the springs from which the fathers drank, or by conversion to another system of beliefs."[5] One might even be reminded of sociologist Maurice Halbwachs's contention that "Collective frameworks are... precisely the instruments used by the collective memory to reconstruct an image of the past which is in accord, in each epoch, with the predominant thoughts of the society," though Halbwachs will not be engaged with directly in this work.[6]

But while restorationism and returning to origins are *normally* synonymous, they are not *necessarily* so. Restorationists can also consciously[7] seek to return to a different time period from the past—to recalibrate, as it were, their restorationist assumptions and establish a new normative baseline.

PRECEDENTS FOR RESTORATIONIST RECALIBRATION

That restorationist Christian movements can seek to recover or reclaim other aspects of the past in addition to the history of the early church has been demonstrated in the work of scholars like Jason H. Dormady, whose fascinating 2011 work *Primitive Revolution* reveals how mid-twentieth century Pentecostals and Latter-day Saints sought not only the restoration of "pure Christianity" but also a return to an earlier and ostensibly more pristine era in Mexican national history. In particular, Dormady argues, these Christians "felt that they participated in a restoration of their nation as defined by the liberal republic of Benito Juarez" who governed from 1858-1872. Interestingly, he notes, Mexican Catholics also engaged in the search for historical golden ages, though they preferred a return to "the order offered by medieval Catholicism" and "a state with a powerful ecclesiastical presence and the domination and division of society by corporate sectors."[8]

A 1968 dissertation by William Mervin Moorhouse also usefully explores how political restorationism has functioned in ways similar to, but for purposes sometimes distinct from, its religious counterpart. Comparing and contrasting the rhetoric of first generation Stone-Campbell Movement members with that of Jacksonian Democrats highlights how both groups employed a "restoration theme" to their own ends. "Coexistent with the birth of" the SCM, Moorhouse notes, "was the rise of Jacksonian Democracy, with its theme of 'restoring' the old republican principles of 'egalitarianism,' 'equal representation,' 'the worth of the individual,' and 'the rights of man.'"[9] Given, then, that restorationism is a flexible enough concept to find employment in both religious and political spheres, it is no wonder that there is also the potential for variation in restorationists' choices of normative historical eras.

A more recent, though no less powerful, example of this kind of recalibration—a key component of a group's historical ecclesiology—can be found in the history of the Emerging Church Movement. Though the ECM is neither a traditionally restorationist fellowship nor connected in any official capacity to the Stone-Campbell Movement, making it an outlier among the groups featured in this work, its members have still participated in the search for an "ancient-future faith" or "vintage faith," to borrow a couple of the more frequently used descriptors. This language, though not quite the same as that used by SCM fellowships, nevertheless illustrates that an often overlooked restorationist strain, albeit one with a different baseline, runs deep throughout the movement's theology. In fact, this modified form of restorationism, which seeks to recover aspects of the premodern Christian past to overcome perceived shortcomings with modernist forms of the faith, serves as one of the key elements uniting an otherwise eclectic assortment of believers. Before actually getting into this ECM recalibration, however, it will be useful to briefly recount the movement's historical origins and development over the last two to three decades.

A BRIEF OVERVIEW OF ECM HISTORY

Because the ECM is such a recent phenomenon, few historians have yet turned their attention to it, although a number of sociologists, theologians, and scholars of religion have done so.[10] Antecedents of the movement can perhaps be found as far back as the late 1960s,[11] but the earliest stirrings of what would become the Emerging Church Movement originated with youth ministry revitalization efforts in the United States during the 1990s.[12] One crucial organization which brought together an impressive slate of future ECM movers and shakers was the Young Leaders Network, which was created by the evangelical Leadership Network to address "the greatest problem of the contemporary church —namely, its lack of being 'contemporary.'"[13] Shortly into this quest, however, disagreement broke out; the parent group, LN, was more concerned with finding practical, methodological solutions to generational differences within the church, while its offshoot, YLN, wanted to focus on the broader implications of the postmodern shift for the future of the church.[14]

Even as YLN came to an earlier-than-anticipated end, many of its former members remained in contact during the years that followed. In 2001, several of these likeminded Christians came together to form the Emergent Village online network as a means of connecting with each other through publishing efforts, conferences, and blogs.[15] A handful of prominent ECM authors and speakers also began to rise to prominence in the broader Christian world around this time. Brian McLaren's 2001 fictional dialogue, *A New Kind of Christian*, did much to publicize the growing movement, selling over 100,000 copies and paving the way for a spate of "emerging" books and book series.[16] Rob Bell, heavily influenced by his reading of McLaren's work, became nationally renowned for works like *Velvet Elvis*[17] and for his NOOMA devotional short films while also serving as pastor of Mars Hill Bible Church[18] in Grandville, Michigan.[19] Scholar of religion Phyllis Tickle has also helpfully overviewed contemporaneous developments in Britain, observing that "of all things, a report written by a committee" in the Church of England played a key role in the development of the ECM parallel movement "Fresh Expressions" during the mid-2000s.[20]

With greater visibility came greater scrutiny, however, and the ECM generated a veritable storm of criticism as its influence grew. Evangelical theologian D.A. Carson's 2005 *Becoming Conversant with the Emerging Church* was the first and perhaps most prominent work to raise various theological concerns about the ECM, but it was by no means the last or the only, with a deluge of books, articles, and dissertations following soon after.[21] Some critics argued that ECM authors like Brian McLaren engaged in theological cherry-picking, "picking and choosing what he likes from among what he dislikes."[22] Rob Bell's *Love Wins*[23] provoked at least two books from other prominent Christian writers for his seeming embrace of, or at least refusal to condemn, universalism.[24] Somewhat more mundanely, Donald Miller, best known for his bestselling *Blue Like Jazz*,[25] ran into a buzz saw of criticism for admitting that he had not regularly attended church services in half a decade.[26] Yet though use of the "emerging" label has declined somewhat in recent years, likely owing in part to such criticism, the influence of the ECM and its leading figures can still be seen today in current manifestations and descendants like the annual Wild Goose Festival—colorfully described on its official website as "a sing and dance and play and dream and eat and camp and meditate and talk and listen and twirl-you-around-and-shake-you-up gathering, born out of the 'Wild Goose' spirit metaphor which is all about beauty, grace, and yes, unpredictability."[27]

Outlining the historical origins of the Emerging Church Movement is one task; actually defining and describing the core tenets of its theology is another. One immediate difficulty is posed by terminology. In ways that will seem quite familiar to members of the various Stone-Campbell fellowships, there has been significant wrangling within ECM circles over the proper nomenclature for the group, or groups, if there is even a group to name.[28] For the purposes of this chapter and project, I have chosen to use "Emerging Church Movement" as a catch-all, umbrella term encompassing those who identify as "emerging" or "emergent," as well as those whose beliefs and practices qualify them as such, even if they might shun the label itself. (In fact, for some, the denial of the "emerging" label paradoxically forms a core part of the "emerging" identity.)[29] I have also opted for "Emerging Church Movement" because of its parallels to "Stone-Campbell Movement" or "Restoration Movement" and because the similarities among its members outweigh the differences, even under this expansive definition.

Having said all of this, a brief diversion into the name debate will work as a suitable introduction to several core aspects of ECM belief and identity. A helpful place to start in this regard is Scot McKnight's 2007 *Christianity Today* article, "Five Streams of the Emerging Church." McKnight, like many other scholars, notes the important distinctions between "emerging" and "Emergent" as descriptors for the group. The former, he argues, is the "wider, informal, global, ecclesial (church-centered) focus of the movement," while the latter, which is effectively the Emergent Village organization mentioned above, "is the intellectual and philosophical network of the emerging movement."[30] (Again, for clarity's sake, my use of "Emerging Church Movement" more closely meshes with the first of these two terms, which includes the second within it.) McKnight goes on to offer five key themes that resonate throughout the larger movement: it is prophetic and provocative in its calls for change; it is postmodern in its rejection of metanarratives, Christian or otherwise;[31] it is praxis-oriented in its desire to live out rather than merely affirm faith; it is post-evangelical in its skepticism toward systematic theology and exclusivist approaches to Christian identity; and it is political in its embrace of a more openly left-wing faith.[32]

Another accounting of the ECM's multifaceted identity comes from former YLN member Mark Driscoll's "A Pastoral Perspective on the Emergent Church." Following theologian Ed Stetzer's lead, Driscoll argues for the existence of three primary "types" within the movement, some of which he finds more palatable than others. First are the "relevants," such as Dan Kimball and Donald Miller, who he describes as "theologically conservative evangelicals... [focused on] updating such things as worship styles, preaching styles, and church leadership structures." Second are the "reconstructionists," who are likewise evangelical in orientation, but who instead prioritize reform to ecclesial models and institutions. This category includes many missional church authors and organizers like Alan Hirsch and Michael Frost and should not be confused with the quite different "Christian Reconstructionist" or "Dominionist" movement associated with R.J. Rushdoony.[33] Last are the "revisionists," like Brian McLaren and Doug Pagitt, theological progressives who "question key evangelical doctrines" and their applicability in a rapidly postmodernizing world.[34] While one might quibble with some of Driscoll's placements today (for instance, Rob Bell no longer seems to fit easily into the first column, though he might have at the time of Driscoll's article), the categories nevertheless highlight crucial variations in the ECM mosaic which McKnight's themes did not address.

Marti and Ganiel's 2014 *The Deconstructed Church*, already cited several times above, loops in a handful of other key aspects of ECM identity which have not yet been mentioned by McKnight or Driscoll. Providing thick descriptions based on visits to each type of setting, the authors argue for the centrality of four different "manifestations" of the ECM: pub churches, Emerging Christian conferences, web-based networks, and neo-monastic communities.[35] Pub churches, they write, provide opportunities for participants to discuss "matters of life and faith," aided by the social lubricant of beer, without the trappings or practices traditionally associated with church settings.[36] Conferences, in contrast to local pub churches, are occasions for ECM figures from across the US (and beyond) to connect with fellow practitioners who are likewise "actively renegotiating the beliefs and practices of mainstream Christianity."[37] Online networks such as Emergent Village provide a third mode of ECM connectivity, allowing for in-depth theological discussion and the distribution of information about conferences, resources, and the like. Finally, neo-monastic communities whose members "either live together in a large house or close to each other in a specific geographical area" aim to meet the needs not only of group insiders but of neighbors who live in the general vicinity of the community.[38]

Regardless of which of these three models, or combination thereof, one attempts to map over the wilds of the ECM, it is clear that the movement defies easy categorization and contains a variety of individual actors and subgroups, not all of whom agree on purpose, terminology, or indeed, even the existence of a larger movement. Nevertheless, that so many scholars and pastors have offered up categorical schemes indicates that there is indeed some sort of "there" there, and by keeping in mind the various characteristics that these experts have identified, along with the brief history given earlier, it is possible to form a reasonably coherent mental image of the ECM for use going forward.

FROM ANCIENT-FUTURE TO VINTAGE AND BEYOND

Of course, one aspect of ECM theology which has not yet been addressed directly in any of the above schema is its modified form of restorationism, which differs from many versions of the doctrine in at least one major aspect: its recalibration of the normative era (or eras) of the historical church. To be sure, several scholars have noted in one way or another that the ECM is less preoccupied with the future (and more connected to the Christian past) than its postmodern lingo and trendy worship gatherings might indicate. American religious historian Steven P. Miller finds that while the ECM's "eclectic and innovative worship styles explicitly repudiated the sentimentalist trappings of contemporary culture," it still largely followed an older playbook of evangelical engagement with and "remixing of" the broader culture for evangelistic purposes.[39] J.R. Franke, in an entry in the *Evangelical Dictionary of Theology*, observes that while critics of the ECM often characterize it as a dangerous step away from the orthodox faith, members frequently appeal to history and "counter that their practices are more faithful to Jesus's way than those of churches influenced by Christendom."[40] More directly, philosopher James K.A. Smith wonders if the ECM "has retained something of modernity's ahistoricism or its evangelical version, primitivism." He likewise notes that the postmodern call to follow Jesus without tradition or denomination can often, somewhat ironically, end up producing "a lingering, disincarnate rejection of time, history, and tradition" not all that dissimilar from the evangelicalism which it seeks to distinguish itself from.[41]

Although I would push back on Smith's inflexible equation of ahistoricism with primitivism/restorationism,[42] I wholeheartedly agree with his diagnosis—that the ECM has, for better or worse, carried with it a version of restorationism which seeks to make an end run around recent Christian history, often labeled "modernism" or "modernity," to an older and apparently more authentic faith from deeper in the Christian past. This prioritization of a "vintage faith," to use Dan Kimball's phrase (analyzed in greater detail below), owes much to the writings of twentieth century theologian Robert E. Webber. Although not necessarily an ECM member in his own right, Webber's formulation of an "ancient-future faith" has made him one of the most significant theological influences on the movement all the same.[43] By the mid-1980s, Webber had begun thinking deeply about why many evangelicals, himself included, were increasingly attracted to more historic churches and liturgical forms of worship. In his 1985 *Evangelicals on the Canterbury Trail*, for example, Webber identified "mystery, worship, sacraments, historical identity, ecumenical affiliation, and holistic spirituality" as six key factors helping account for the shift, while also affirming that evangelicals moving into the mainline world would bring with them "experiences that can contribute to the spiritual life" of their new ecclesial homes.[44]

Among Webber's clearest statements along this line of inquiry came in 1999 with *Ancient-Future Faith: Rethinking Evangelicalism for a Postmodern World*. According to Webber, "the challenge of the church in the postmodern world is to recover community within the local church and the community of the entire church throughout history."[45] This historical search for community, to be sure, is not a straightforward pattern-oriented restorationism; yet simply forsaking the past altogether is hardly a preferable option for Webber. What is necessary instead, he argues, is the rediscovery of a "universally accepted framework of faith" stretching from the apostles through the Fathers and down to the present day. Apparent in Webber's thinking here and elsewhere are 1) a sense that modern forms of Christianity alone were insufficient in an increasingly postmodern world; and 2) a belief that the premodern Christian past could provide a viable faith which could take root in the "rich cultural context" of the pluralistic present day.[46] Each of these views, whether directly stated or indirectly implied, have played significant roles in shaping ECM historical ecclesiologies by opening the door for a recalibration of the normative Christian past, allowed ECM members to draw widely from the broad sweep of premodern Christian history.

Scholars and ECM members alike have written about the ECM's adoption of aspects of premodern Christianity. "This return to the past should not be confused with a nostalgia for 1950s Protestantism or with a circling of the wagons and a purer Reformation theology," Scott Bader-Saye has written in the *Christian Century*. "The return is deeper, looking to the treasures of the medieval and patristic theologies and to practices that have long been ignored by evangelicals."[47] Doug Pagitt, a figure whose involvement in ECM circles dates back to the Young Leaders Network of the 1990s, similarly claims that "Saying the words of those who lived and worshiped in the second century places our faith in the context of something bigger than our time and our concerns."[48] And Patrick Malloy, writing in the *Anglican Theological Review*, notes that "Emerging Christians have rediscovered ancient practices, especially patristic practices, and are using them to attract postmodern people and inspire conversion, not only of intellectual belief (if even of intellectual belief), but of life."[49]

One term used by some within ECM circles to describe this orientation is "vintage faith." Pastor and author Dan Kimball has perhaps done the most to articulate this concept—not trying to turn back the clock for nostalgia's sake, but returning to the stores of the past in order to find long-forgotten treasures for the present and future. "In the cases of wine and clothing," he writes in 2003's *The Emerging Church: Vintage Christianity for New Generations*, "vintage refers to the high quality or value of something old. I think the same goes for the disciplines of our faith."[50] Rather than relegating the old to the dustbin of history merely because it is old, Kimball and other ECM leaders have found ways to incorporate it into new ways of being and believing. In *Emerging Worship: Creating Worship Gatherings for New Generations*, published the following year, Kimball concisely illustrates this tendency when he notes that "In Vintage Faith Church, we use an eclectic blend of the ancient with contemporary pop."[51]

In 2006, pastor and theologian Ray S. Anderson released *An Emergent Theology for Emerging Churches*, which, almost from the beginning, adopts Kimball's "vintage faith" terminology to describe an orientation which is "not a form of modern theology, nor is it merely postmodern" but is instead "intended to remind emerging churches of their origins and lead them forward to fulfill their destiny to expand God's kingdom..."[52] The emphasis on the inherent value and usefulness of the riches of the Christian past for the Christian present and future runs throughout the work. Two pages later, Anderson notes that in reading Kimball's writings, "the word *vintage* took me back, not to something that was good *merely* because it was old but to what was true and authentic because it was there in the beginning and points the way into the future."[53] Later, he cautions against what he sees as a dangerous tendency within ECM circles to abandon the "vintage gospel" and not merely the "older wineskins [which] have carried it forward in history," in favor of a less substantial and less satisfactory "new wine."[54]

Erin Theresa Wyble's 2006 dissertation also briefly notes the presence of the "vintage faith" concept within the ECM, even describing it in terms that correctly identify its restorationist bent. She argues that "in many ways adherents to 'emerging' conversations imagine revitalizing and restoring (at least evangelical) Christianity." Despite the movement's "novelty and its postmodern approach," she contends, the presence of "vintage faith" language indicates "efforts to return to a previously more pure Christianity—a golden era of discipleship (that likely exists only in imagination)..."[55] Regardless of one's perspective on the existence and nature of that golden era, Wyble has helpfully if tentatively identified a link between the "vintage faith" motif and the larger world of restorationist Christianity.

EMERGENCE AND RESTORATION: LOOKING AHEAD TO MOVE AHEAD

Another important wrinkle for the "ECM as restorationist" thesis is that ECM authors and leaders often describe Scripture not as a single set of blueprints to be restored but as a narrative of emergence which is instructive for today's Jesus followers who, like the original believers, live in a time of great cultural upheaval. Indeed, the proliferation of sets of blueprints, or models, is a key defining aspect of the ECM. Dan Kimball notes that "Instead of one emerging church model, there are hundreds and thousands of models of emerging churches."[56] Rob Bell, in the aforementioned *Love Wins*, adds that Christian orthodoxy itself contains a multitude of views and voices, offering present-day believers an example of discourse, discussion, and disagreement rather than a single model to implement in their own time:

> ...nothing in this book hasn't been taught, supported, or celebrated by many before me. I haven't come up with a radical new teaching that's any kind of departure from what's been said an untold number of times. That's the beauty of the historic, orthodox Christian faith. It's a deep, wide, diverse stream that's been flowing for thousands of years, carrying a staggering variety of voices, perspectives, and experiences.[57]

Freed from the need to identify a single correct set of doctrines to export from the first century and import into the twenty-first, therefore, ECM leaders instead draw parallels between the attitudes and general experiences of earlier Christians and those of believers today. Brian McLaren notes that the desire for emergence shaped and reshaped the faith throughout its first centuries: "It caused ancient Christians to emerge from first-century Judaism. It caused their descendants to emerge from apostolic Christianity to the era of the martyrs and apologists, showing both courage and intelligence in dealing with their evolving situation."[58] Similarly, ECM fellow traveler Phyllis Tickle connects what she identifies as an ongoing "Great Emergence" to earlier paradigm shifts in Christian history, such as the "Great Reformation" a half millennium earlier: "about every five hundred years the empowered structures of institutionalized Christianity, whatever they may be at that time, become an intolerable carapace that must be shattered in order that renewal and new growth may occur."[59]

THE ECM RECALIBRATION OF THE NORMATIVE CHURCH ERA(S): LOOKING BEHIND TO MOVE AHEAD

Even though this prevalent narrative of emergence serves an important role in ECM identity formation, members have still frequently continued to appeal to premodern Christian history, including but not limited to the early church, for examples of beliefs, practices, and ways of being which, they feel, have been overlooked in the modern era. This somewhat more freewheeling approach to the past has in turn led many scholars to overlook or downplay this ECM restorationist strain. Yet this search for an "ancient-future faith" or "vintage faith" stills fits the bill of restorationism in that it 1) seeks to overcome the present flaws and omissions of a more recent Christian era (in this case, of "modernity" or of "modernism") by 2) making an end-run around that time period to the more distant Christian past and recovering aspects of that past to resource the present and future church.

First, the ECM rejection of what it labels "modern" or "modernist" forms of Christianity is one of only a handful of aspects which unifies an otherwise heterogeneous movement. This self-consciously postmodern stance has already been identified above, though a number of scholars not cited there have made similar claims about the centrality of postmodernism in ECM thought. For instance, Kate D. Simcox writes in her 2005 dissertation that the ECM "critique of 'modern' Christianity entails a rejection of systematic, hierarchical, individualistic, consumer-driven models of religious praxis."[60] Likewise, Karyn L. Wiseman has made a compelling case for the impact of "postmodern architecture's playfulness, exuberance, and cultural sensitivity" on the worship spaces created and adapted by ECM gatherings.[61] Additionally, McLaren biographer and scholar Scott R. Burson notes that while "the real issue for McLaren is not postmodern epistemology," it does still function as "a means to an end" in helping foster conversations about "the ethical implications of postcolonialism."[62]

The ECM desire to avoid the trappings of modern/ist[63] Christianity has also been identified by several Christian theologians and pastors ranging from supporters to skeptics. D.A. Carson, whose aforementioned *Becoming Conversant with the Emerging Church* critiqued numerous aspects of ECM theology and practice, nevertheless admitted that "there is something very refreshing, on the one hand, about not being bound by tradition – after all, isn't Scripture itself supposed to be our only *final* guide? – and, on the other, about wanting to be linked to historic Christianity and not merely the latest twenty years of Christianity."[64] On a related note, megachurch pastor Rick Warren, who contributed several sidebars to Dan Kimball's *The Emerging Church*, suggested that

> Unfortunately, many who want to return to the 'ancient faith' don't want to go back far enough. They only want to go back to the architecture and rituals of the Dark Ages, when the church was the most ingrown and least missional. My prayer is that we'll go all the way back to the New Testament, where they used homes, not Wal-marts or cathedrals. *That* is vintage faith![65]

Though Carson and Warren might not see eye-to-eye with ECM leaders as to the merits of the ECM "vintage faith," they are nevertheless in agreement that those leaders were seeking to draw from a much longer swath of Christian history in their efforts to revitalize the church in the present day.

More directly relevant to this project, William R. Baker, in a 2008 pair of articles in the *Christian Standard*, identified seven points of similarity between the ECM and the SCM, including the reality that both "[leap] over the doctrinal and denominational battles of later centuries" in an attempt to recover "the earliest, clearest expressions of Christianity."[66] Graham Bates, in an unpublished research paper from 2014, argued that both movements "removed their generation's bridge keeper separating non-Christians (and many Christians) from God and His church"—for the SCM, the bridge keepers were divisive creeds, but for the ECM, the bridge keeper was the institutional church itself.[67] That same year, Elesha Coffman, writing for the *Religion in American History* blog, noted similar parallels between the two movements as she read through Marti and Ganiel's sociological study *The Deconstructed Church*.[68]

Evidence of the ECM stance towards modern/ist forms of

Christianity can, of course, also be found in the writings of ECM leaders themselves. Donald Miller, for instance, laments what he sees as a general lack of self-questioning in recent Christian history, observing that "if it *was* a religious system that explained the human story, its adherents had lost the grandness of its explanation in exchange for its validation of their *how* lifestyles..." Drilling down, Dan Kimball argues in *The Emerging Church* that "what we need to do in the emerging church is to rethink what aspects or values of modernism became more or less accepted standards, rather than Scripture, for how we go about ministry."[69] Similarly, in his follow-up volume *Emerging Worship*, he adds that "As we begin to question why we do certain things we need to pay attention to the origins of our Christian worship practices. We will often find some startling similarities and contrasts between what 'church' was to the early Christians and what we think it is – or long for it to be – today."[70] Eddie Gibbs and Ryan K. Bolger's *Emerging Churches: Creating Christian Community in Postmodern Cultures* confirms that ECM members "demonstrate a strong commitment to the Bible as their guide for the journey but are seeking to read it with fresh eyes as they shed the constrictions of modernity and endeavor to apply the story of God's redemptive engagement with humankind in a cultural context that raises new questions and poses fresh challenges."[71] Brian McLaren chimes in optimistically that while ECM participants have "begun to seek a fresh understanding of what Christianity is for," they have likewise discovered "that a lot of what we need most is already hidden in a trunk in our attic."[72]

A number of notable ECM authors, including McLaren and Nadia Bolz-Weber, were raised in restorationist churches, and at least at times, they have spoken fondly of those experiences. McLaren has commended groups like his native Plymouth Brethren for having "a beautiful, childlike desire to follow Jesus whatever the cost and however lonely the road."[73] Bolz-Weber, raised in Churches of Christ, has somewhat more begrudgingly acknowledged that "for all its nonsense and obsession with being good and alienation of people who weren't their particular *brand* of 'good,' the Church of Christ I was raised in was a community."[74]

Not content to air grievances with modern/ist forms of Christianity, then, ECM authors also seek to reclaim practices and beliefs from the premodern eras of the faith, stretching from the early church through its medieval descendants. James Bielo's *Emerging Evangelicals*, one of the earliest scholarly works on the ECM, concisely describes the wide-ranging nature of this return to the past: "closer attention to the annual church calendar...; designing multisensory worship experiences; performing monastic disciplines; integrating pre-Reformation theologians into public and private reading rituals; and rethinking the role of materiality in worship events" all manifest the ECM's awareness and use of the past.[75] Brian McLaren, in *The Secret Message of Jesus*, brings together an unlikely assemblage of heroes from the broad geographical and temporal sweeps of Christian history, writing that "Often, after an especially bad season of disappointing performance when the art of the kingdom is nearly lost, a new master musician will arise and reinfuse the tradition with vitality and passion – a St. Patrick, a St. Francis, a Teresa of Avila, a Hildegard of Bingen, a John Wesley, a C.S. Lewis, a Desmond Tutu, a Mother Teresa."[76] Rob Bell similarly appeals to a "long tradition of Christians who believe that God will ultimately restore everything and everyone," a tradition which, he asserts, includes Peter, Paul, Clement of Alexandria, Origen, Gregory of Nyssa, and Eusebius, among others. "At the center of the Christian tradition since the first church," he contends, "have been a number who insist that history is not tragic, hell is not forever, and love, in the end, wins and all will be reconciled to God."[77]

To be sure, Bell warns elsewhere against a strict back-to-the-early-church restorationism, a refrain that has likewise been sounded by many within ECM circles. In his 2017 *What is the Bible?*, Bell cautions that "behind this statement" lurks a mythical or idealized version of the early church, rather than a useful and usable model for the church of today: "But reading the Bible, you learn that it's not about trying to be something you're not – it's about learning to see the movement and motion and possibilities right in the midst of whatever world you find yourself in."[78] Yet Bell has also affirmed being "part of [a] tradition" of those who, like Martin Luther, were "*reforming*" (emphasis his) the church. A rejection of pattern-oriented restoration of the early church did not entail a rejection of the need to dig through the stores of the past to find overlooked resources for the church of today.[79]

Again, this kind of recalibration of the normative historic era(s) of the Christian past necessarily implies the existence of some form of restorationism within the ECM identity, one which has also manifested itself in the movement's practices and worship styles and not simply in its writings. Nadia Bolz-Weber, whose upbringing was in Churches of Christ, provides a powerful example of the ECM recovery of ancient forms of worship in a postmodern context. "As Kate and

Megan sang the ancient chant," she writes of a service that took place at the Denver-based House for All Saints and Sinners, "it felt as though their voices were reaching through two thousand years of Christian faith and bringing back into the room with them the full force of humanity's folly..." [80] Sounding a similar note, Sally Morgenthaler, contributing to Dan Kimball's *Emerging Worship*, distinguishes between modern, "disenchanted worship [which] is about human units in their individual padded seats" and the kind of "historic worship [which] is first and foremost about God..."[81] In the same book, Kimball notes that "emerging churches use crosses, that usually look ancient,"[82] while in the predecessor volume he asserts that "in church architecture in the past, the choir was often placed in the rear of the building, which eliminates any sense of performance or focus on the singers."[83] Brad Harper and Paul Louis Metzger, in their introductory work on ecclesiology, confirm these ECM tendencies toward employing the ancient in the present when they write that "the emergent church... uses icons in worship, enhancing their sense of participation in the ancient drama of salvation as it unfolds in the contemporary world."[84]

But the desire to draw from the wellsprings of the premodern Christian past to strengthen the church of postmodernity goes beyond décor. Leonard Sweet describes his 2007 work *The Gospel According to Starbucks* as an "attempt at updating the medieval method of reading for the four senses of Scripture (literal, allegorical, tropological, and analogical) and applying these four senses to the reading of culture."[85] Sweet also stresses the importance of multisensory experience to premodern Christians, seeking to recover such in the present day. He vividly describes to the reader "the smell of burning incense and beeswax candles, the sound of bells big and small, the touch of a fingered rosary or *benatier*, the taste of the Eucharist or Festival foods, the sight of tapestries and secret misericords, not to mention postures, gestures, ritual acts, mystery plays, passion plays, and town processions" as just some of the sensory experiences which brought the Christian faith out of the head and into the world.[86]

CONCLUSION

Though the Emerging Church Movement differs quite substantially from the three groups featured in the other chapters of this work, a modified restorationism (often under the guise of an "ancient-future faith" or a "vintage faith") has played an important role in its theological history all the same. Even as the ECM has experimented with new forms of worship and other practices in an attempt to keep itself relevant in a rapidly changing postmodern culture, it has also adopted and adapted many aspects of premodern Christianity which, members argue, have been overlooked by an overly intellectualized and overly rigid modern form of the faith.

This rummaging through the cupboards of ancient Christianity, different as it is from Alexander Campbell's "search for the ancient order," meets the standards for restorationism in that it identifies shortcomings in recent manifestations of Christianity and seeks to address those flaws by looking to the distant past, recovering beliefs, practices, and other tenets of that ancient faith for the benefit of Christians living in the present and future. That ECM authors and leaders feel at liberty to draw on a longer swath of Christian history does not exclude them from the restorationist camp. Rather, it shows how malleable the restoration ideal can be. Not only do restorationists differ in their approaches to reading Scripture (as we have seen in the previous chapter), they can also differ in the normative baselines that they seek to restore. Even though this aspect of historical ecclesiology is not always directly addressed—for most restorationist groups, the unquestioned assumption is a restoration of the early church, which is often simply equated with the New Testament church—foundational assumptions matter immensely, and even minor changes to those assumptions can lead to very different results in different restoration "projects."

3

REPLICATION

In recent years, scholars working in a wide variety of scientific and social scientific disciplines have had to wrestle with what is commonly called a "replication crisis" concerning the ability to confirm and create indisputable "facts." The full scope of this epistemological emergency is only starting to come into view, but the crisis consists of at least two components. First, despite the widespread belief that confirming experimental results by reproducing them under identical conditions is what "distinguishes scientific from nonscientific research," there has been comparatively little interest among academics in attempting to duplicate or disprove the results and conclusions of other experts. Historian and philosopher of science and economics Philip Mirowski has stated succinctly that "in the history of science, it is rare to find actual replications; and in many of the paradigm instances they were never even tried."[1]

This general dearth of replication attempts has itself

obscured the second, perhaps even more troubling, aspect of the crisis: the difficulty, if not outright impossibility, of fully replicating the conditions of an initial experiment. Again, Mirowski notes that "one of the main findings of science studies is that replication of every possible step of a procedure is uncommon in most science because one cannot banish the local contingency within any complex experiment."[2] Mirowski is neither a lone wolf nor the boy who cried wolf in this instance. A team of medical researchers has recently suggested that flipping a coin is roughly as effective as attempting to replicate a study, at least when the original experiment's "initial effect [was] barely significant...."[3] John P.A. Ioannidis's provocatively titled essay "Why Most Published Research Findings Are False" likewise warns of the dangers of "claiming conclusive research findings solely on the basis of a single study assessed by formal statistical significance..."[4] Popular outlets including the *Atlantic*, *Vox*, and *FiveThirtyEight* have also published stories on the replication crisis, bringing this somewhat heady discussion to a larger audience.[5] Although the exact diagnoses and solutions that these and other observers offer vary widely, there is clearly an increased level of concern that one of the scientific method's bedrock principles is less securely entrenched than previously thought.

The difficulty of replicating past events and outcomes is old hat, though, to the many restorationist Christians who for centuries have been attempting to duplicate the doctrines, practices, and structures of the early church in their own days and ages. Despite the many challenges these believers have faced in so doing, their conviction that the contemporary church has an *obligation* to replicate the early church is necessarily built on the underlying assumption, stated or otherwise, that it also has the *ability* to do so.[6] Members of many restorationist traditions have often shared a high degree of certainty about the replicability of the early church. An unusual example of this conviction can be found in an undated pamphlet by Christadelphian author and apologist Ron Abel which seeks to answer the following inquiries:

> Is it essential that hats be worn by sisters today when social custom has changed so much? If they should be worn, when? At the Memorial Service only? Or whenever a sister prays, even when giving thanks for a meal? Such questions have arisen in the minds of many thoughtful sisters. Perhaps, too, some of the brethren have found difficulty in providing perfectly consistent answers.

Abel acknowledges that divining scriptural guidance on these matters is not easy, particularly given that "modernistic clergymen" in other Christian groups "have been vocal in support of 'women's lib' and often foremost in dismissing the teaching of the Apostle Paul as 'anti-feminist' and 'retrogressive.'" Nevertheless, New Testament teachings on head coverings, he asserts, are recoverable and replicable in the present day despite this broader cultural shift.[7]

Although the replicability of the early church's example is a separate concern from the exact substance of its theology and praxis, restorationists' views on replication are nevertheless crucial in shaping their respective historical ecclesiologies because they help determine which aspects of the early church's example are binding (or at least beneficial) for believers today. As we will see shortly, conflicting beliefs about the Holy Spirit and the profound differences in the cultural contexts of first- and twenty-first-century Christianity have frequently put restorationists' core conviction regarding the replicability of the early church to the test. In some cases, restorationists have been able to resolve these issues by divining an underlying biblical principle, rather than a specific pattern of action, to be restored. But in other instances, restorationists have been forced to tacitly admit that some aspects of the first-century faith simply could not be replicated by later generations—an admission usually made, however, without conceding the larger point regarding the early church's replicability in toto.

"...A CONCESSION TO THE EVIL PRINCIPLE OF DEMOCRACY": COMING UP SHORT IN THE REPLICATION OF THE EARLY CHURCH

Sometimes, the obligation to replicate the early church is described as ongoing participation in a process, rather than as total completion of a set task. For instance, in the April-May-June 2001 issue of *Think On These Things*, a periodical associated with non-institutional Churches of Christ, editor Al Diestelkamp offered a word of caution to those brothers and sisters who thought of restoration as a fixed goal to be achieved—or, even more dangerously, as a fixed goal that had already been achieved. "Somewhere along the way," he wrote, "some of the beneficiaries of this struggle [to restore the early church] began to think of the restoration as having been accomplished." Instead, Diestelkamp continued, restoration should be thought of "as an ongoing process of spiritual growth... our task is to be restoring *ourselves* to Christ-likeness."[8]

Conversely, longtime Texas preacher J. Early Arceneaux, writing over fifty years earlier in the *Gospel Guardian*, then the flagship publication of the non-institutional Churches of Christ, implied that it *was* possible for Christians to fully live up to the standards set by the early church. This thorough replication was feasible despite textual errors in individual biblical manuscripts and the great difficulties inherent to the translation process.[9] Arceneaux noted that Jesus and his disciples "quoted from a very imperfect translation of the Old Testament"—the Septuagint—yet still accomplished their respective God-given missions. Likewise, the author observed wryly, "If Christ could use an uninspired and imperfect translation, we can too, and not suffer too much damage." Not content to leave the matter there, Arceneaux added, "the Book we read today is substantially identical with the writings of the apostles." There would be no valid excuse—none granted by the biblical texts, at least—for the modern-day believer who failed in his or her mission to replicate the first-century faith.[10]

For Diestelkamp, replication of the early church was an ongoing process; for Arceneaux, a fixed goal to be fully achieved. Yet despite this variation in their respective historical ecclesiologies, the two men agreed that was possible for Christians to fully participate in the project of replicating the first-century faith—to meet whatever obligations were incumbent on them as restorationists. They concurred as well that the Scriptures were sufficient guides for Christians in all generations and that the patterns of church governance and right living contained within could be accessed by believers in the present. Twentieth-century Christians, like all others, would fall short from time to time, but with prayer, study, and hard work, they could fruitfully work toward restoring the early church in their own era.

Yet, as mentioned above, restorationists have sometimes been forced to admit that the early church might not be fully replicable, at least in specific aspects, in their own era. Again, such acknowledgements have not usually negated believers' broader convictions regarding the replicability of the early church as a whole, but these thorny theological thickets have often posed considerable challenges for restorationists all the same. One area in which contemporary circumstances have frequently conflicted with restorationist assumptions about the replicability of the early church is the matter of church governance. Believers in both Christadelphian ecclesias and non-institutional Churches of Christ have struggled to reconcile the apparent absence (or at the very least, redefined role) of the Holy Spirit in the present day with New Testament descriptions of direct divine selection of church leaders in the first century. Their attempts to reconcile modern experiences with biblical precedents reveal their deep-seated convictions about the replicability of the early church but also show their equally strong belief that the work of the Holy Spirit had in some way changed over time or ended altogether.

In 1883, Robert Roberts, the de facto leader of the Christadelphian movement during its second generation, penned a treatise on church governance known today as the "Ecclesial Guide." Roberts, working in an era of Christadelphian history characterized by sustained numerical growth but punctuated by bouts of theological schism,[11] sought to encapsulate in a short pamphlet the biblical pattern for the "foundation and conduct of ecclesias." (Christadelphians prefer the use of "ecclesia" in place of "church" when referring to an individual congregation of believers, holding that the latter term has been irrecoverably sullied through abuse and misuse by other Christians.)[12] As Christadelphian founder John Thomas had done throughout the decades before, Roberts directly appealed to apostolic precedent time and time again throughout the manual. The Christadelphian movement, Roberts argued, "has been perfectly natural in its proximate features... but thoroughly spiritual and apostolic in its results."[13] Apostolicity, per the usual, was the gold standard for the Christadelphians.

However, Roberts also acknowledged a difficulty posed by the seeming absence of the Holy Spirit in his own time:

> In our own day, until the Spirit speaks again, we can have no such privilege; and it is worse than useless to profess a possession we lack. Our wisdom lies in recognizing the true nature of our case, and making the most of the unprivileged circumstances of a time succeeding to a long period of divine absence and eclesial [sic] chaos.[14]

In the wake of John Thomas's tireless study of the Bible, the Christadelphians had brought about a "revival of the original apostolic faith" in the nineteenth century.[15] But while the style and substance of the early church had returned, the Spirit had not. Indeed, the full title of Roberts's guide—*The Truth in the Nineteenth Century: Or, the Lessons of Thirty Years' Experience Presented in the Form of a Guide to the Formation and Conduct of Ecclesias, in the Characteristic Circum-*

stances of an Age When the Truth as Apostolically Delivered has been Revived in the Ways of Divine Providence, Without the Co-operation and Living Guidance of the Holy Spirit as Enjoyed in the Apostolic Age—acknowledged as much. "Truth" had been "revived," but believers would nevertheless have to make do without the Spirit.

In and of itself, the absence of the Holy Spirit would appear to put a wedge between nineteenth-century believers and their first-century counterparts. But the Spirit's ostensible departure during an earlier age of apostasy also posed a related issue for Christadelphians regarding the replicability of biblically-authorized church governance in the modern age. "If God would speak, as in the day of the Spirit's ministration," the process of selecting ecclesial leaders would be both straightforward and scripturally sanctioned. Yet "God is silent," Roberts conceded, and "there is no alternative but to make the best appointments we can amongst ourselves, aiming in all things to come close to His mind and will, as expressed in the written word of the apostles." Roberts dejectedly added that heeding the will of the majority in this matter was "doubtless a concession to the evil principle of democracy" but that no better solution had presented itself.[16] For the Christadelphians, then, ecclesial governance provided a specific area in which a larger theological commitment to the replicability of the first-century faith was pushed to its limits, and perhaps beyond, by a competing theological commitment—in this case, a cessationist view of the Holy Spirit.[17]

Another attempt to reconcile these two convictions appears, however, in the early 1940s writings of Foy E. Wallace Jr., at that time a leading figure within the non-institutional Churches of Christ.[18] Wallace sought to resolve the apparent tension between the two beliefs by showing that there was really no tension at all. Instead, he argued in the pages of the *Bible Banner*, the equally alliterative predecessor of the *Gospel Guardian*, direct divine involvement in the appointment of church leaders during the apostolic era was the historical exception, not the rule. Divine attestation to the authority of the apostles and other early church leaders, Wallace contended, was only necessary because the first Christians did not yet have access to the entirety of the Spirit-inspired written Word of God. "This order of apostles, prophets, pastors, evangelists, teachers, was designed to safeguard the church against error in the absence of the revealed word," he wrote, nothing more than a temporary system to shepherd the flock while the Scriptures were being written and collected. "But when 'that which is perfect' (I Cor. 13) was come"—i.e., when the New Testament was completed—there would be no need for such direct intervention.[19]

For Wallace, the biblical pattern of church governance, properly understood, was eminently replicable by modern believers. This pattern, this "permanent organization of the church," included but three categories: elders, deacons, and church members. (Preachers were explicitly not part of congregational leadership but were instead to concern themselves with preaching the gospel.) This system was in no way inferior to its predecessor, wrote Wallace. In fact, if properly replicated by believers, it would work perfectly: "If this divine plan fails to function, the fault is not with the plan, but with our own failure to respect it and work it. The plan is perfect because it is God's..." Believers were incapable of devising a better system of church governance, Wallace ultimately concluded, but they would certainly be able to follow the divinely established pattern from Scripture.[20]

Foy E. Wallace Jr. was not alone in believing that the biblical pattern for church governance, properly understood, was fully replicable in the twentieth century. His brother, Cled E. Wallace, shared this firm conviction and defended it on a number of occasions in the *Gospel Guardian*. In fact, Cled argued in 1949, so thorough were the Scriptures that they even provided the proper nomenclature for present-day believers to use in speaking of the church. "If a man is of the New Testament variety," according to Cled, "then New Testament brands would serve to identify him." Conversely, "if he has to be called something else to identify him, it must follow that he is something else... [and that his behavior is] unscriptural, not according to the will of God and the source of about all the trouble and division there is in religion."[21] Full replication of the biblical pattern required the use of biblical language, but this replication was well within reach because of the Spirit's full provision of the appropriate terminology for church offices and practices within the Scriptures.

Together, the writings of Robert Roberts and the Wallace brothers illustrate how different facets of believers' historical ecclesiologies—such as a belief in the total replicability of the early church and a parallel belief that the Spirit's work in the church had changed or concluded since the first century—could create tensions which needed to be resolved in some form or fashion. For some, such as Roberts, the appropriate response was simply maintaining both beliefs anyway, acknowledging the difficulty of doing so, and making the best of a tough situation. For others, such as Foy

E. Wallace Jr., the friction disappeared when the actual biblical pattern was properly discerned and the peculiarities of early Christian experience were identified for what they were. Both approaches remain part of the movement oeuvre to this day.

Other challenges in replicating the early church in the present day would arise not from difficult-to-reconcile beliefs but from the undeniable reality that modern life differed greatly from the cultural context in which the Bible was written. These kinds of difficulties might be answered, restorationists discovered, through the rediscovery and replication of an underlying biblical principle rather than the apparently more straightforward restoration of a simple biblical pattern.

"THE CHURCH IS A KINGDOM": RECOVERING BIBLICAL PATTERNS—AND PRINCIPLES—OF CHURCH LIFE IN THE INTERNATIONAL CHURCHES OF CHRIST

Convictions regarding the replicability of the early church have also been tested by the contextual differences separating, for instance, the Jerusalem of the first century from the Los Angeles of the twentieth. The International Churches of Christ have faced these challenges on a number of fronts. Members of the ICOC have responded, in some instances, by asserting the continued existence of a binding biblical pattern that believers simply must implement today, cultural changes notwithstanding. But in other instances, they have aimed to overcome the difficulties posed by contextual differences by recovering an underlying biblical principle that could be replicated regardless of the specific geographical, temporal, or other circumstances faced by believers.

Skepticism about democracy, at least in the realm of church governance, has appeared frequently in the official publications of the ICOC and its predecessor movements, just as it has in many Christadelphian writings. Unlike the Christadelphians, however, members of this fellowship continued to assert the replicability of the early church's organizational hierarchy in a modern context; there would be no concessions to the "evil principle" here. One theological variation between Christadelphianism and the ICOC which made this assertion more feasible was the latter group's contention that the Holy Spirit was indeed still present in the lives of its members. This conviction (and the related assertion that God was actively helping modern believers rediscover long-lost theological truths) narrowed the distance between first- and twentieth-century experiences and laid the groundwork for the church's teachings about the replicability of a more authoritarian hierarchy in a modern democratic context.

For instance, in the May 1988 *Boston Bulletin*, the leading publication of the ICOC forerunner "Boston Movement," prominent teacher and elder Gordon Ferguson argued that even though God was not "continuously revealing spiritual truths," He was certainly active in revealing "the *application* of those old truths."[22] This revelation, according to Ferguson, had led to a more authentic replication of the early church than had previously been known: "In short, the biblical plan is again being followed and biblical results are again being produced."[23] Specific aspects of this plan which had only recently been revealed, recovered, and replicated, asserted Ferguson, were "church plantings, with a focus on one church per city, every-member evangelism, discipleship partners, training of ministers through discipling relationships, women leading women, church reconstructions, disciple's baptism, and evangelists discipling elders."[24]

Yet despite the heavenly helping hand which had made it possible to restore these biblical patterns, some Boston Movement and ICOC writers would acknowledge that contextual circumstances outside the four walls of the church had changed since the first century, making it difficult to fully replicate other patterns set by the early church. Although these contextual changes would not shake members' certainty that they could replicate the first-century faith in their own time, believers would have to reckon with those differences all the same. Sometimes, they would do so by doubling down on strict adherence to the biblical pattern regardless of the level of difficulty; in other cases, the rediscovery and replication of a more fundamental biblical principle undergirding a pattern of behavior would make it possible to restore the early church in a significantly different cultural context.

One specific area in which leaders and members would take the former tack, refusing to budge from what they saw as a mandatory biblical pattern, was in the realm of church governance—a matter which had also posed a challenge to Christadelphians and to members of non-institutional Churches of Christ. In a 1987 article series titled "Authority and Submission," church elder Al Baird defended the church's strict standards for personal conduct and its demands for nigh-unquestioning deference to church hierarchy. Baird was well aware that many church members would be culturally conditioned to favor a more democratic system of church government, particularly those Americans believers whose backgrounds had been in the congregationally-governed Churches of Christ. Yet there was no need to compromise biblical teachings on ecclesiastical authority, Baird asserted.

> Democracy is a great form of civil government, but there is no scriptural basis for thinking that church policies are to be determined democratically. The church is a kingdom with its style of government established long before our Western democracies were born.[25]

The cultural circumstances of the United States, including its electoral politics, varied significantly from those of the Roman Empire during the first century. Nevertheless, biblical teachings were clear: the church was to more closely resemble a monarchy than a democracy. Baird, like many others, would continue to argue in the years to come that "throughout the pages of the Bible and history God raised up one person to lead his people"—and, on a related note, that in the present age, this person was undoubtedly Boston Movement and ICOC leader Kip McKean.[26]

Many of Baird's contemporaries in the ICOC also spoke about their shared conviction that biblical patterns could, and should, be replicated in many areas of Christian life. Theologian Sarah Dannemiller, in an unpublished paper on gender roles within the Boston Movement, has argued that the teachings of "prominent female Boston leader" Patricia Gempel were typically supported "with multiple examples from Scriptures, as was appropriate for a movement rooted within a restoration tradition."[27] Similarly, group members Sheila Jones and Terrie Fontenot each contributed entries to a 1996 volume reflecting this underlying restorationist assumption. Jones, for her part, asked her readers, "Why do we sometimes not greet each other 'warmly in the Lord' as Aquila and Priscilla greeted the Corinthian church?"[28] Fontenot likewise warned her audience that mere physical presence at church services was not enough: "we can violate this scripture [Hebrews 10:25] and still be present because the admonishment is not just to be there, but to 'encourage one another.'"[29] Church members may not have been greeting or encouraging each other as they should have been, but this was fixable, because they certainly had the ability to do better.

But even leading figure Al Baird would be forced to acknowledge that some cultural changes could inhibit a strict restoration of biblical patterns of authority, necessitating the replication of an underlying biblical principle instead. For instance, one major difference separating the twentieth-century United States from the first-century Roman Empire was that legally sanctioned slavery no longer existed in America by that time—to say nothing of the differences between the former American and Roman systems of slavery themselves. "The closest thing most of us have to a master-slave relationship today is the employer-employee relationship," Baird wrote in the previously mentioned 1987 "Authority and Submission" series, referring to the Apostle Paul's admonitions to first-century Christians who lived in a world thoroughly dominated by Roman slavery. Yet he still sought to unpack the deeper truth contained within Paul's teachings of submission to a higher authority, a principle that would remain relevant to working American believers in the late 1980s. Ultimately, Baird concluded, "the same principles apply—obedience, respect, fear and sincerity of heart. Our work is that done for Christ, not just to win the favor of our boss."[30]

Authority and submission were not the only theological areas in which church members sought out deeper biblical principles to be replicated in their own cultural contexts. A key plank of the ICOC historical ecclesiology has been the oft-repeated assertion that the early church had achieved a high degree of racial, ethnic, cultural, linguistic, or some other type of integration. These kinds of unity would comprise a major goal for modern-day church members, but the specific demographic circumstances of the first-century church differed notably from those of its twentieth-century progeny. Believers would need to figure out the Bible's guiding principles on such matters and then seek to live them out in their own specific contexts around the world. Several scholars from the social sciences have already investigated aspects of this ICOC distinctive. Sociologist Kathleen E. Jenkins, for instance, argued in 2003 that high-boundary religious movements like the ICOC often seek to create settings of "intimate diversity" to foster in-group connections between persons of widely varying backgrounds.[31] Another sociologist, Gregory C. Stanczak, reached a similar conclusion three years later regarding the "strategic ethnicity" of the ICOC—the church's public presentation of its apparent multiracial and multiethnic harmony as evidence for the truth of its other teachings.[32] Political scientist Joseph Eugene Yi, in the meantime, had also observed how various religious groups in Chicago, including the ICOC, effectively "combine[d] authoritative tradition with interracial outreach." In this respect, he noted, such groups resembled institutions such as karate schools, which likewise blended older traditions (often transported to the United States by specific immigrant communities) with an "individualist and plural" willingness to welcome interested persons from a wide variety of backgrounds.[33]

But the ICOC desire for a harmoniously multiracial and multiethnic fellowship of believers at both the congregation-wide and movement-wide levels was not *just* a marketing ploy (though it may *also* have been one). Rather, the church's oft-stated desire for such integration was rooted deeply in its historical ecclesiology—specifically, in its teaching that the early church was likewise integrated in ways that were progressive, even counter-cultural, in its day and age. This conception of the early church permeates the writings of many members of the ICOC and its predecessor movements alike, including a number of articles featured in the pages of the *Boston Bulletin*. In an extended article series stretching across several months of late 1986, missionary Scott Green encouraged *Bulletin* readers to seek inspiration in the unifying ministry of Paul—in particular, the apostle's missionary journeys into the "Greco-Roman secularized world" which reflected the early church's "new vision for global evangelism."[34] A week earlier, Green had similarly argued that "Jesus' perfect strategy" of public preaching "included deliberate forays into the core fellowships of Palestinian Jews," highlighting the Lord's own conscientious efforts to heal divisions and bring unity to a fractured body.[35] Green would go on to offer readers a distinctly restorationist chiding in a later entry in the series for overlooking "the soaring example" of the early Christians, whose "lifestyle of public preaching and teaching" had been abandoned by modern believers in favor of evangelizing in "less threatening scenarios."[36]

ICOC (and predecessor movement) authors also occasionally acknowledged, however, that while the early church's focus on integration across various boundaries could provide a general principle to be replicated in the present, the specific cultural circumstances of modern believers around the world could vary drastically from those of the first Christians. For instance, high-ranking church official Jaime L. DeAnda contributed an article to a 1987 issue of the *Boston Bulletin* which focused almost exclusively on the goal of intra-congregational integration. "Sometimes we forget that the church of Acts 2 was a multilingual church," he wrote, and "we also need to accept the fact that there will be special needs among Christians of different ethnic groups." Present-day believers should not despair at this reality, DeAnda continued. They should instead follow the example set in Acts 6 by the apostles themselves, who appointed deacons in the Jerusalem congregation to make sure that the Greek-speaking widows were not ignored in the church's benevolent efforts by program overseers who primarily spoke Hebrew. The culturally astute Paul would also provide a tailor-made example for DeAnda, just as he had for Green: "Like Paul's Greek ministry in Jerusalem, the Spanish-speaking community provides today's church with an excellent base for mission training." Naturally, the specific linguistic contexts of present-day churches differed from those of the Jerusalem church, but the underlying principle of targeting charitable and evangelistic efforts to meet the needs of sub-communities within individual congregations could (and should) certainly be replicated.[37]

Similar appeals to the first-century faith likewise appeared in *L.A. Story*, the monthly bulletin of the Los Angeles Church of Christ, which served as the flagship paper of the ICOC during the 1990s. (In this respect, it replaced the *Boston Bulletin*, which had functioned in a similar manner for the Boston Movement during the previous decade.) The October 8, 1995, "Mi Familia" issue in particular promoted the church's worldwide mission efforts among a wide variety of nations and people groups. Church elder Al Baird admitted in an editorial that "Growing up I never even had any acquaintance [sic] who were Black, Latin, [or] Asian." Baird's affiliation with the ICOC, however, had changed all of that. "Today I have friends from more nations than I can count. I live in Los Angeles, a city of incredible diversity. Now I understand what Paul wrote in Galatians 3:28, 'There is neither Jew nor Greek, for you are all one in Christ Jesus.'"[38]

Nor were ICOC efforts to foster multiracial and multiethnic harmony confined to the United States. Missionary and ICOC official Mike Taliaferro, describing the church's early 1990s evangelistic outreach in South Africa, claimed that "when a South African walks into our Sunday service [in Johannesburg] he sees something he's never seen before. He sees 1400 people—half black, half white—happily praising God together." A photograph of young children of varying skin tones accompanying the article is given the short caption, "The church nursery—where race doesn't exist."[39]

Even more obvious examples than these appeared in the

church's April 1999 bulletin, which highlighted ICOC efforts to break down racial barriers worldwide. Al Baird's editorial contained the assertion that "one distinguishing mark of God's modern day movement"—a designation used often by ICOC writers to refer to the ICOC itself—"is the obvious love that we have for one another." This love does not come easily or cheaply, Baird acknowledged: "We who have looked down on others and somehow thought we were better must repent," while "those who have been hurt by the results of racial hatred must forgive and trust again." But this was nothing less than the standard to which Jesus called the church, Baird concluded.[40]

The apparently successful replication of this biblical principle of integration was demonstrated to readers via a collection of short mission reports from ICOC congregations from around the world. One paragraph tells the story of Thomas Augustine, described as "a black man with former gang ties" who joined the L.A. congregation after a period of Bible study. "This brother," the report continued, "who was taught never to trust white people, shocked family and friends from the world with a white best man at his wedding and a 'rainbow coalition' wedding party." The San Diego congregation, by contrast, included a former "skinhead" who had "repented of her racial hatred when she read about the love of God and later married a Latino brother." The Berlin church was home to three women, two of Turkish background and one of Kurdish descent, who had become close friends despite their past prejudices. Similar examples from congregations in the Philippines, the Dominican Republic, Curacao, Lebanon, Singapore, Syria, Japan, and Ireland, as well as in Chicago,

Illinois, and Charlotte, North Carolina, were included as well.[41]

Given what we know about the ICOC's use of "intimate diversity" and "strategic ethnicity" as evangelistic tools, it may be reasonable to question just how representative such stories were of the typical experiences of most church members. But our concern here is the church's historical ecclesiology and, more specifically, its members' stated desire to replicate the biblical principle of multiracial and multiethnic harmony as seen in the example of the early church. On that matter, the picture is clear. Despite the notable contextual differences posed by distance in both time and space, ICOC authors frequently held up as instructive the early church's purposeful efforts to foster unity across racial, ethnic, cultural, linguistic, and other lines—as well its efforts to right wrongs (as in Acts 6) when they occurred. To be sure, ICOC members also demonstrated their awareness that the cultural contexts of a Boston or a Los Angeles differed from those of a Jerusalem or a Rome. Yet for these and many other authors and leaders within the ICOC, the underlying principle remained recoverable and, more importantly, replicable by the church of the present day.

CONCLUSION

The restorationist ideal has sometimes been styled as full participation in an ongoing process, at other times as the completion of a clearly-defined project. In either case, restorationists have necessarily shared the underlying assumption, whatever the specifics of their historical ecclesiologies may have been, that the early church is indeed replicable in the present day. Yet this conviction has been tested on a number of fronts—by apparently incompatible beliefs, such as a strictly cessationist view of the Holy Spirit, and by the not-inconsiderable differences between the first- and twenty-first-century worlds. In some instances, believers continued to assert the existence and replicability of divinely sanctioned patterns, while in other circumstances, they were forced to acknowledge the infeasibility of those patterns and/or to seek out underlying (replicable) biblical principles.

Whether defined as principle, pattern, project, or process, the assumption that the early church remains replicable in some form or fashion constitutes an important component of all restorationists' historical ecclesiologies, or conceptualizations of the early church. As we have already seen, however, the definition of the "early church" has been a point of great contention in its own right. Some restorationists have sought to restore it using only what information is contained in the New Testament; others have pushed well beyond this point, consciously recalibrating their definition of the early church to include a much broader swath of time and, potentially, a much longer list of things to restore. Restorationism can take a self-referential turn, too, as believers unconsciously start to seek a return to their own specific movement's point of origin, or another golden age from its past, alongside a return to the era of the early church. This unwittingly recursive restorationism will be the subject of our final chapter.

4

RECURSION

To this point, our discussion of historical ecclesiology in and around the Stone-Campbell Movement has emphasized variables which relate specifically to restorationists' conceptualizations of the early church—their understandings of the Bible's revelations about it, their occasional recalibration of its temporal bounds, and their convictions regarding its replicability in the present day. Another key aspect of historical ecclesiology, however, is that there is a strong propensity within restorationist fellowships to add their particular movement's origin story as a second set of blueprints to restore. To be sure, restorationists rarely equate the two eras and almost never state a desire to restore the church of the nineteenth or twentieth century. Nevertheless, they do frequently hold up their movement forebears as worthy of emulation, idealizing the past and finding the present lacking in comparison.

So while such groups do continue to seek to restore first century Christianity, they often stop far short as they travel back through time, landing in the nineteenth or twentieth century instead. To describe this trend, I am adopting and adapting a term from the worlds of linguistics and computer science: recursion.[1] Although the term can and does take on a variety of highly specific meanings in different academic contexts, my use of the term is most similar to that of computer scientist and philosopher Douglas Hofstadter. In his most famous work, *Gödel, Escher, Bach: An Eternal Golden Braid*, Hofstadter defines recursion as "nesting, and variations on nesting. The concept is very general. (Stories inside stories, movies inside movies, paintings inside paintings, Russian dolls inside Russian dolls (even parenthetical comments inside parenthetical comments!)—these are just a few of the charms of recursion.)"[2]

I argue that members of restorationist traditions display a recursive tendency when they begin idealizing or pining for a return to the good old days of their own movement, whenever those days may have been, and thereby define their project in terms of restoring their own restoration movement's history, rather than in terms of restoring the early church. Restorationism remains paramount when this shift occurs, to be sure, but the exact substance of what is being restored changes, and in ways not always immediately apparent to adherents themselves. The predisposition of a movement to seek a return to its own origins likely grows stronger over time, but we will also see that the recursive tendency can develop in a very short period—no longer than a couple of decades. Additionally, it should be noted that these groups are not somehow unique in idealizing their own respective histories. The point, in fact, is that they are not. If these groups—some of which are relatively young, and each of which differs notably from the others—have all manifested the recursive tendency, then it stands to reason that other restorationist fellowships have done so as well.

One scholarly study which has hinted at this trend within Churches of Christ is Gary Holloway's *Saints, Demons, and Asses: Southern Preacher Anecdotes*, which shows how members of the fellowship in later generations often drew on idealized versions of prominent historical figures for inspiration.

> Following the time that the initial leaders of the Restoration Movement died, it became customary to enshrine the works of prominent preachers in a biography, usually published shortly after their death. All of the stories here come from biographies written by members of the movement; most are not by professional historians. Their tone is extremely hagiographic. In spite of these limitations, they do present anecdotes of certain preachers that were in common use soon after their deaths.[3]

Holloway's point that most of the works were written by amateur historians and chroniclers is well taken. But even though the movement's lay biographers frequently succumbed to the temptation to hagiographize their forebears, they were concerned enough with their movement's history to commit a version of it to paper—belying the notion that restorationists are ipso facto uninterested in past events outside of the New Testament and indicating an underlying belief that their fellowship's past could be worthy of imitation.[4]

Again, such engagement by restorationists with their

movement's history, flawed as it sometimes has been, runs counter to interpretations which stress the supposedly ahistorical nature of restorationist theologies. That participants in the Stone-Campbell Movement have, at times, been quite indifferent toward their own past is undeniable. Earl West, in the preface to the second volume of *Search for the Ancient Order*, writes that "there is something merciless in our ability to forget the heroes of the past, and their battles for truth... what Sir Thomas Browne calls, 'the iniquity of oblivion.'"[5] Similarly, Kerrie Handasyde, in exploring the creation of historical myth within Churches of Christ in Victoria, Australia, notes that the congregational polity of the fellowship has led to a "rewritten, concealed, contested" history in which supposed "great men" play an outsized historiographical role; yet even they, as Handasyde notes, often "remain unfamiliar in modern Churches of Christ."[6] Yet it is also important to remember, as Seth Perry has usefully reminded us, that the "historylessness" of the Stone-Campbell Movement has been greatly overstated.[7]

Not only did these early Disciples understand their model church—the early church—to be historically rooted; members of subsequent fellowships in and around the Stone-Campbell Movement have understood them, and their respective groups' founders, as instructive examples of real people accomplishing real things in real time. This chapter will explore recursions within each of our three SCM fellowships in turn and then finish with some tentative conclusions about recursions which already appear to be manifesting within the comparatively young Emerging Church Movement. This approach will allow us to better see how, for instance, Christadelphians in later generations looked back not only to the early church of the first century but the early Christadelphians of the nineteenth.

RECURSIVE RESTORATIONISM IN THE CHRISTADELPHIAN MOVEMENT

As the oldest of the fellowships under consideration, it is no great surprise that Christadelphianism offers some of the clearest examples of recursive restorationism. While recent Christadelphians have often fought over the meanings of their forebears' teachings—and about which of those forebears eventually left teachings worth fighting over—there has nevertheless been in practice a general consensus that the writings of earlier generations should be studied and their actions emulated.

PIONEER PERSONALITIES

During the First World War, Frank G. Jannaway, a leader in the South London ecclesia, became perhaps the single most influential Christadelphian as he successfully lobbied the British government for total exemption for combatant and noncombatant service.[8] In 1920, after the war's conclusion, Jannaway went on to publish *Christadelphian Answers on All Kinds of Difficulties, Objections, Arguments, and Questions, Exhibiting "The Truth" in Opposition to the Dogmas of Papal and Protestant Christendom* as a compilation of orthodox Christadelphian teachings for use in personal study and debate with nonbelievers.

Like John Thomas and Robert Roberts before him, Jannaway remains on high alert against clericalism. "With larger numbers in the ecclesias," he notes, there is a correspondingly greater risk of "the development of a considerable body of 'non-workers' who leave the proclamation of the Truth and other features of the Truth's warfare too exclusively to the duly appointed serving brethren."[9] Many of Jannaway's other descriptions of the early church sound familiar as well. He contends that "care and discrimination were enjoined upon the First-century brethren" in selecting officeholders within the local ecclesia.[10] The guidelines for selecting those leaders, Jannaway argues, "are definitely and clearly laid down in the New Testament."[11] And "although there is no express command that we should observe" the Lord's Supper weekly, "all the information in the Scriptures at least suggests such periodical observance thereof."[12] Like Christadelphian leaders before him, then, Jannaway assumes that the combination of direct commandments and apostolic precedents offers a clear picture of the early church, which believers in his generation can and should follow.

Crucially, however, the first century is not the only era to which Jannaway hearkens back. Writing nearly a century after John Thomas's fateful trip from Britain to the United States and over two decades after Robert Roberts's death, Jannaway occasionally speaks about the early Christadelphians as he does the early church, portraying them as a people more in tune with God's will than those in his own time. For Jannaway, the lives of those Christadelphian pioneers merit close study because they, like the apostles, were the guardians of Truth:

> "Yet they, being dead, speak"—speak to a new generation of Christadelphians, who know little of the fierceness of the early combat, or of the spirit of the earlier brethren and sisters. Young brethren and sisters—and older ones, too—may well ponder carefully their sterling words when confronted with the allurements and temptations of modern times, remembering that it was their faithful and uncompromising attitude in both doctrine and practice which has resulted in our receiving the precious heritage of the Truth in its purity and simplicity...[13]

To be sure, Jannaway never argues that Thomas and Roberts were inspired by the Spirit in the same manner as the apostles. Thomas may have been "absolutely devoted to a disinterested exposition" of the Bible; yet careful study and hard work, not miraculous wisdom, made him the leader that he was. And Roberts's chief contributions, including the "establishing and building up of ecclesias throughout the English-speaking world," seem more secretarial than spiritual in Jannaway's estimation.[14]

Even so, Jannaway makes it clear that something important had been lost since the halcyon days of the founders. Equally clear in Jannaway's mind, too, is that the careful study of the founders' writings could forestall the "spirit of compromise" besetting believers in his generation and restore Christadelphianism to its past glories. "As an antidote," Jannaway writes, "this book gives the mature judgment of leading Christadelphians." If "those Ecclesias presided over by brethren who have not made a special study of [Thomas's writings] are of a Laodicean type, and have very poorly attended audiences at all their meetings," then the solution is quite simple: read the works![15] And rather than handing out as Sunday School prizes through "thoughtlessness, or incompetency, or something worse" such dangerous works as *Gulliver's Travels* and *Jane Eyre*, ecclesias should give children page-turners like the "Life of Robert Roberts" instead.[16]

From the interwar period on, Christadelphians the world over alternated between major schisms and unsuccessful reunifications.[17] Those who were frustrated by the divisiveness never lost sight of the first-century church, of course, but they also sought guidance in the examples of earlier Christadelphians. For instance, Harry Tennant, author of *The Christadelphians: What They Believe and Preach*, connected his own efforts to "set forth in writing the content" of Christadelphian belief with earlier undertakings by John Thomas, Robert Roberts, and notable post-World War Two leader John Carter who, Tennant claimed, all held a "common faith" across the decades.[18]

In contrast to Jannaway's characterization of those "pioneers" as fierce warriors for the faith, others saw them as having been essentially united in belief and unity-minded in practice. In 1973, Christadelphian author and missionary Harry Whittaker wrote a lengthy two-article investigation of the controversial teaching of "block disfellowship"—the belief that proper ecclesial discipline requires breaking ties with heretics and with those congregations which fail to publicly denounce them, even if those ecclesias hold no unorthodox views themselves. The articles display a continued devotion to restorationism in that the imitation of the first century church is their stated goal. Yet they also demonstrate a recursive tendency in their appeals to the lives and teachings of earlier Christadelphian believers.

At the outset of the first article, Whittaker, one of Christadelphianism's "leading contemporary interpreters" during his lifetime, establishes the pattern of the early church as the standard for believers in his day, just as his Christadelphian predecessors had done.[19] "That the heretic himself should be the subject of ecclesial discipline is not in question," according to Whittaker. "[T]he teaching of the New Testament is clear enough on this."[20] Less clear, however, is if those who personally hold orthodox beliefs but fail to condemn heresy should be subject to discipline as well. In other words, should the whole "block" of those who neglect to disfellowship heretics be disfellowshipped themselves? Though "certain vociferous minorities insist that the existence of one heretic in a world-wide group of ecclesias... makes them all unfit," Whittaker claims that "it is not Biblically certain that such a man (or ecclesia) deserves the drastic cutting-off which some would rush to apply."[21]

Whittaker continues by systematically examining the passages often cited in support of block disfellowship, finding that those scriptures "have been misapplied... in order to put on a pseudo-Biblical footing a conclusion for which there is no adequate foundation."[22] This abuse of the apostolic precedent does not mean that there is another, more appropriate standard, however—far from it. "[T]here are certain New Testament passages which seem to show with unmistakable clearness that the apostles reserved their censure and acts of ecclesial discipline for men who were false teachers," Whittaker asserts, and he offers several examples in support of this interpretation. For instance, he notes that the Apostle Paul, when confronted by some who denied the resurrection of the dead, in no way threatened to disfellowship them. Rather, he "reason[ed] solidly, persuasively, simply—so simply, in fact, that one marvels at his patience."[23]

Like Frank Jannaway before him, Whittaker also argues that the writings of the early Christadelphians—not just those of the early Christians—can offer guidance to believers in his generation, if only they would take the time to read.

> The situation is all the more tragic because for many years there has been available in the Constitution (respected by all, and followed by most) a concise statement of sensible procedure by which to cope with problems of just the kind discussed in this study... The brethren who first framed these words showed wisdom. A careful pondering of them makes it very evident that this procedure and the principle of "block disfellowship" cannot exist together.[24]

But Whittaker's conception of the pioneers differs from Jannaway's in at least one crucial respect. Whereas Jannaway portrays Robert Roberts and the other early Christadelphians as brash and confrontational users of "uncompromising language," Whittaker presents them as longsuffering, unity-minded, and reluctant to divide.[25] A half-century's worth of schism had, it seems, transformed the original Christadelphians from iconoclasts into irenics.

WHO COUNTS AS A CHRISTADELPHIAN?

A significant debate also raged within twentieth-century Christadelphian circles over who, exactly, qualified as a past leader. Could anything be learned from those who lived during the many centuries between the apostolic age and John Thomas's rediscovery of the truth? Were there individuals or even entire groups who covertly held Christadelphian doctrines? Or had correct belief completely vanished from the Earth for over a millennium and a half? All parties involved agreed that men like John Thomas and Robert Roberts were worthy of imitation, at least in most respects; they differed greatly, though, as to whether or not present-day Christadelphians would find fellow believers (and, presumably, suitable role models) further back in the historical record.

That John Thomas and (to a somewhat lesser extent) Robert Roberts were to be admired, even imitated, was almost universally accepted across the Christadelphian world. Even J.J. Andrew, who broke sharply from his contemporary Roberts over the issue of "resurrectional responsibility," sought to frame his position as more loyal than his opponent's to the views of John Thomas.[26] Writing in 1895, Andrew admitted that his own beliefs were not entirely the same as Thomas's, yet accused Roberts of having selectively quoted the founder's words to support erroneous teachings. "In order to make it appear that Dr. Thomas is in entire harmony with the present teaching of *The Christadelphian*," Andrew wrote of Roberts's paper, "two quotations have been made... from his writings... But the purport of the Doctor's argument has been misapprehended."[27] Roberts, Andrew continued, "has done more to mar the work of Dr. Thomas than anything which has occurred since the Doctor's death." And Andrew's own divergence from Thomas's conclusions was solely, according to Andrew, the result of his firm faithfulness to Thomas's principles:

> It is solely because of adherence to the Scriptural teaching set forth by Dr. Thomas that I have, in carrying that teaching to its logical conclusion, been led to differ from him on resurrection to judgment.[28]

Even in dissent from the specific position staked out by Thomas, then, Thomas's teachings remained the gold standard for Andrew.

Yet there has been much less agreement as to whether "the faith" actually existed between the apostolic era and Thomas's day and age. Islip Collyer, in *Letters to Young Christadelphians*, asserts that "our doctrine of the Kingdom of God was a point of orthodoxy throughout the whole of the Western Church for the first three centuries of the Christian era."[29] Alan Eyre's controversial work, *The Protesters*, goes even further, claiming that

> the Christadelphian community... is the inheritor of a noble tradition, by which elements of the Truth were from century to century hammered out on the anvil of controversy, affliction and even anguish.[30]

Even if "[s]ome recorded herein perhaps did not have 'all the truth,'" Eyre contends, "[i]f one does not know more of the truth at the end of one's pilgrimage than at the beginning or the middle, then he is a poor disciple indeed."[31]

Others have been less persuaded. Responding directly to Eyre's work, Ruth McHaffie notes her "surprise that the individuals who had been identified and accepted as 'our brethren'" in *The Protesters*, "though holding some doctrines in agreement with ourselves, differed widely on others."[32] She later adds that if a modern-day Christadelphian held the same views as some of Eyre's examples, they would be "seen as perverting the Word, and [would be] deemed to be outside our Lord's household."[33] Thomas Gaston, writing in the *Christadelphian eJournal of Biblical Interpretation*, builds on McHaffie's work by examining the teachings of supposed "proto-Christadelphians" in light of the modern Statement of Faith. He concludes that the "Waldenses alone of all the groups we have considered had significant parallels with modern Christadelphians" and that the Donatists, Nestorians, and Cathars would have been quite hostile to, rather than permissive of, Christadelphian doctrine.[34]

Although these and other Christadelphian authors disagree about the likelihood of finding true believers in the post-apostolic, pre-Thomas historical record, there is nevertheless a general consensus that the experience of the first century church is not the only usable past for modern-day restorationists. Christadelphians who find kinship with the Waldenses or Cathars or some other group seek to emulate the tenacity of those men and women who, they believe, held to the truth despite living in an era of general apostasy. Christadelphians who see such groups as heretical in their own right, by contrast, make John Thomas seem even more worthy of imitation, because his rediscovery of biblical doctrine would have been correspondingly more difficult (and his efforts more important) in the absence of a tradition of true believers. Either way, all sides agree implicitly that looking to the more recent past, not just the age of the apostles, can be a useful and fruitful endeavor for modern believers seeking to revitalize the faith in their own time.

RECURSIVE RESTORATIONISM IN THE NON-INSTITUTIONAL CHURCHES OF CHRIST

Like the Christadelphians, members of the non-institutional Churches of Christ have sometimes looked back into their own, more immediate past, not just to the story of the early church, for examples to emulate and realities to restore. Like the Christadelphians and members of the International Churches of Christ, they have not always agreed about how far back their own history goes. Nevertheless, many within the fellowship have shown a real willingness to characterize their forebears within the Stone-Campbell Movement (and within the non-institutional congregations more specifically) as examples of how modern Christians should behave and believe.

HISTORICAL THINKING AND THE NON-INSTITUTIONAL CHURCHES OF CHRIST

Though from a historical perspective the roots of the non-institutional Churches of Christ clearly wind back through the soil of the Stone-Campbell Movement, some members have, for a number of important reasons, not always been eager to see themselves as part of a larger historical restoration movement. For instance, in 2001, Al Diestelkamp offered a thoughtful critique of the restoration motif from the non-institutional perspective, distinguishing between a perceived need for restoration at a movement-wide level and an actual need for restoration at the individual or congregational level. "The church that Christ built needs neither renovation nor restoration," he contends. "You can't restore what is already perfect. What we *can* restore is ourselves and the local congregations of which we are members. In other words, the restoration process is not a brotherhood project."[35] A half-century earlier, Fanning Yater Tant went even further, decrying the use of "Church of Christ" as an adjectival phrase—"'church of Christ people,' 'church of Christ preachers,' 'church of Christ doctrine...'" To many within the wider world of Protestant Christianity, such usage might seem entirely harmless, but Tant warned that "the churches of the Lord are becoming filled up with Ashdodish[36] expressions and sectarian ideas." The use of the phrase, he continued, implies that those true "churches of the Lord" are nothing more than one denomination or movement among many, rather than the unique gatherings of New Testament Christians that they are called to be.[37]

However, other figures within non-institutional circles have been more willing to acknowledge their connection to a larger fellowship or historical restoration movement, even though they might still find fault with their predecessors on various points of doctrine. Melvin Curry, for one, has argued that while those of previous generations were not perfect, they sought after laudable goals all the same:

> In a nutshell, they pointed to the Bible as the old paths! So how can we find fault with what they did in pointing to the old paths unless we have a problem with the concept of the old paths itself. We should admire the men of the Restoration Movement of the early nineteenth century for their willingness to correct the errors into which the bypaths of denominationalism had led them and through 'a restoration of the ancient order of things' to walk once again in the right way of the old paths.

In Curry's estimation, then, the key contributions of these first-generation members of the movement were their rejection of denominational identity and their recognition that the Bible provided everything necessary to restore the New Testament church. Both of these qualities, Curry argues, are worthy of emulation in the present, even if he contends elsewhere in the same lecture that "I am content to stand with the Lord and His apostles.... What better guides could we have to lead us back to the old paths?"[38]

During the same 1990 Florida College lectureship at which Curry spoke these words, Hoyt Houchen called to mind the parallels between the early-twentieth-century division of Disciples of Christ from Churches of Christ and the mid-twentieth-century split within Churches of Christ—both of which stemmed, at least in part, from the same issue of inter-congregational missionary efforts. Speaking of his involvement in the latter division, Houchen notes, "Some of us who have been on the firing line can sympathize with those brethren who opposed the Missionary Society in the last century." Like those who spoke out a half-century earlier against the ACMS and were "branded 'antis'" for their efforts, members of Houchen's own generation "have received the same treatment." Yet Houchen, it seems, finds strength in the power of their examples: "We do not have the 'crying towel' out. Such is expected when brethren stand for the truth."[39] Similarly, Fanning Yater Tant published a biography of his father, J.D. Tant, in 1958. Characterizing the older Tant as someone engaged in a "battle for the truth [which] shall never be completely won, nor completely lost, until the last trump shall sound," Fanning Yater encourages his readers to take up that same fight. "In doing so they will prove themselves worthy fellow-workers with that great host of godly men who have preceded them," he contends, "and who shall follow them, in the greatest calling among men."[40]

A powerful example which pushes much further back in time can be found in the writings of minister and professor Homer Hailey. Hailey, writing in the *Bible Banner* in 1941, noted the importance of "battles... waged by Campbell, Stone, the Sewells, Lipscombs, and hundreds of others" but also those of Protestants and proto-Protestants like "Savanarola, Martin Luther, Zwingli, John Knox, and others..." To be sure, Hailey admits of Savanarola and company, "we agree not with their doctrinal positions." Nevertheless, he continues, "we cannot but admire the valor of these men" and should strive to learn from both their shortcomings and successes in order "to stem a tide of digression and apostasy" in the modern age.[41] So while there has not always been complete uniformity of belief about which previous generations of Christians were worthy of emulation, members of non-institutional Churches of Christ have all the same turned their gaze to the more distant past in search of a usable history.

A MID-CENTURY RECURSION

Besides looking back to the history of the larger movement (or an even earlier time) for inspiration, members within the non-institutional congregations have found laudable principles and practices in the mid-twentieth-century origins of their own separate fellowship. A common recursive refrain is that those preachers and writers of the mid-twentieth century were, to put it simply, made of tougher stuff than the leaders of later generations. Writing in *Watchman Magazine* in 1997, Harry R. Osborne decries the general failure of those in his day to condemn Homer Hailey's supposedly unorthodox teachings on divorce and remarriage.

> From pulpits to dining room tables, from Bible classes to college campuses, from 'gospel papers' to preachers of repute, a growing cry is being heard for tolerance of 'diversity' in doctrine and practice, even when sin is involved. It began its current momentum from brother Ed Harrell's plea for continued acceptance of brother Homer Hailey despite his teaching and application of error on divorce and remarriage (*Christianity Magazine*, Nov. 88, pp. 6-9). It gained steam when none of the editors of that paper challenged brother Harrell's error. The speed of the movement increased further when esteemed brethren stepped in to defend the concept that we should praise our 'historical practice' of accepting those who teach some doctrinal errors and practice some sins. It has clearly gone beyond the sound (2 Tim. 2:13; 1 Tim. 6:3f) barrier as some have now begun to praise our doctrinal diversity as a proof of rightful congregational autonomy.

In this section, Osborne strongly condemns what he sees as a misapplication of biblical teachings on (and his fellowship's tradition of) congregational autonomy. Although he does not cite specific historical examples from outside the pages of the New Testament, he does seek to make the case that Christians in any generation (including his own) have the same responsibility as Christians in the first generation: "to study the truth, preach it, and contend with those who promote error." Far from being weaklings who countenance heresy, modern-day Christians are called to participate in a "Warfare [which] is never pleasant, but [which] is necessary."[42]

Similarly, Hoyt Houchen has argued that "Our faithful forefathers fought for every inch of the ground which we now occupy. Therefore, we must be resolved not to relinquish one iota of this sacred ground."[43] And Tom Roberts (like Osborne, writing in *Watchman Magazine*) has admiringly described the perseverance of those who were called "'brotherhood controllers,' 'church splitters,' 'orphan haters,' 'Guardian-ites,' and much worse" for their opposition to institutionalization. "What the preachers and papers did," Roberts claims, "was to furnish individuals and congregations with Bible study and discussions in an open forum that allowed truth to be heard." While such did not go out of their way to be confrontational, neither did they shy away from difficult truths, even if those beliefs forced them to make equally difficult decisions.[44]

In any event, we can clearly see that members of non-institutional Churches of Christ have drawn inspiration from, and even sought to imitate, those from earlier generations of the non-institutional fellowship, of the Stone-Campbell Movement, and even of Protestant and proto-Protestant Christianity. As with the Christadelphians, this recursive restorationism has never replaced members' desire to be like the early church, but it has shaped those efforts towards restoration and influenced how members of non-institutional congregations see themselves vis-à-vis other Christians.

RECURSIVE RESTORATIONISM IN THE INTERNATIONAL CHURCHES OF CHRIST

Though theirs is one of the younger fellowships featured in this book, members of the International Churches of Christ have also frequently engaged in recursive restorationism during their movement's short history. It is worth noting that —as was the case for the other fellowships—members have not always agreed with one another as to when their movement was actually born. Did ICOC history begin with the first stirrings of the Stone-Campbell Movement in the nineteenth century? With Chuck Lucas's adoption of discipling techniques at the Crossroads Church of Christ? With Kip McKean's 1979 rise to power at the Lexington (later, Boston) Church of Christ? With the renaming of his movement in the early 1990s? (Or, as members of the breakaway International Christian Church/Sold-Out Discipling Movement might argue, with McKean's return to prominence in Portland in the mid-2000s?) Despite this lack of consensus, these same members have found within their movement's past, however defined, a usable history and a secondary set of blueprints for their restoration project.

SOMETHING OLD, SOMETHING NEW

As is the case in many restorationist traditions, members of the International Churches of Christ have offered a number of historical interpretations of when, exactly, their movement began. Several ministers and authors within the ICOC (and its predecessors, the Boston Church of Christ and the Crossroads/discipling movement) have claimed Stone-Campbell Movement history as part of their own group's heritage. In an editorial for the first issue of *Biblical Discipleship Quarterly*, a magazine published by the Boston Church of Christ, Marty Wooten argues that the publication "owes its existence to the revived commitment of many to the restoration of New Testament Christianity." He further claims that he and his fellow believers "have a great respect for those who have gone before us—men like the apostles Paul and John, Alexander Campbell, Barton Stone, David Lipscomb and many others." That Wooten would list only men from the early church and from early generations of the Stone-Campbell Movement indicates a clear affinity for the latter on his part.[45]

Later that same year, in the bulletin of the Boston Church of Christ, Bob Gempel offered an interpretation of church history based on the principle that God has periodically called out a remnant of faithful followers from a larger, corrupt church structure to be His chosen people. The Protestant Reformation was just such an event, as was the later Restoration Movement. Gempel notes as well that "we in the churches of Christ see ourselves in turn as a remnant of the Restoration Movement" and implies that the Boston

Movement therein likely constitutes another called-out remnant within Churches of Christ.[46]

Like Gempel, other ICOC writers have criticized previous generations of the Stone-Campbell Movement for failing to live up to their God-given potential. Prominent teacher and ICOC leader Gordon Ferguson (who, like many top ICOC figures, had a background in Churches of Christ) exemplifies this tendency when he compares the experience of the ICOC breaking away from Churches of Christ to the first century experience of Christians breaking away from Judaism.

> However, without question, we owe much to the Restoration Movement conceptually, just as the first century church owed much to the Jewish movement. Frankly, due to their persecution by the Jews, it was not easy for our first century brothers to appreciate the good things from Judaism. Similarly, due to the persecution by mainline Churches of Christ (which has been some of our *worst* persecution), it has not been easy to appreciate the foundational backdrop which we have received from them.[47]

Even though Gempel, Ferguson, and others sometimes keep their Stone-Campbell heritage at arm's length, they nevertheless still identify and acknowledge that heritage as part of their own.

Another frequently referenced starting point for ICOC history is the ramping-up of campus ministry efforts within mainstream Churches of Christ. Churches of Christ, like many other Christian fellowships in the U.S. South and elsewhere, focused their collective attention on college campuses in the post-World War Two era, when enrollments swelled to record levels and aging congregations began to seek infusions of younger members. One of the most remarkable (and most successful) efforts was located at the Crossroads Church of Christ in Gainesville, Florida, home of the University of Florida. This ministry, led by Chuck Lucas, established a new paradigm for campus ministry. Lucas combined earlier organization Campus Evangelism's focus on college outreach with a set of "discipling" techniques developed by charismatic Christian groups to form a one-on-one mentoring system which encouraged all members to share their faith regularly and held them personally accountable if they did not.

Though controversial, this approach led to unprecedented rates of growth at Crossroads, which grew from 275 members in 1970 to nearly four times that number in just seven years.[48] As a result, Lucas came to be seen as something of a campus ministry guru; some Churches of Christ throughout the United States even began sending their ministers to Crossroads to be "discipled," or trained, by Lucas. By 1980, there were at least fifty such Crossroads-trained ministers working in Churches of Christ nationwide. And while Lucas's discipling program was unorthodox by Churches of Christ standards, his theology was by-the-book restorationism, perhaps even more conservative than that found in many non-Crossroads churches.[49]

Lucas's ministry has been described by several ICOC (and predecessor) writers as the start of a new movement. One such instance comes from the preface to Jerry Jones's 1988 evangelistic work *Back to the Basics*. Jones, who was at the time affiliated with the Boston Movement, expresses his gratitude toward the "Crossroads Church of Christ in Gainesville, Florida, for its pioneering efforts in campus work and in training others. Its tape ministry provides a wealth of material for returning to the 'basics.'"[50] Another closely related example can be found in the writings of Thomas A. Jones's 2007 memoir *In Search of a City: An Autobiographical Perspective on a Remarkable but Controversial Movement.* Jones, who played a crucial role in the publishing efforts of the Boston Church of Christ and later the ICOC, notes his roughly forty-year involvement as "an observer of and participant in the movement that culminated in the group known as the International Churches of Christ (ICOC)." Counting back four decades from the book's 2007 time of publication brings one to the late 1960s, the era of Campus Evangelism, and Jones later confirms the short-lived organization's influence when he writes that a 1968 campus ministry seminar he attended was "what would seem later to me to be the birth of a movement."[51]

Sometimes, though, the writer's balance shifts even further, implying (or stating outright) that Kip McKean's arrival in Lexington, Massachusetts, constitutes the real origin of the ICOC. In *Bible-Carrying Christians: Conservative Protestants and Social Power*, David Harrington Watt observes regarding the Philadelphia Church of Christ (an ICOC congregation) that members "were not too interested in the Church of Christ qua the Church of Christ. They were far more interested in the church as an outpost of a larger movement, one that was sometimes referred to as International Churches of Christ (Boston Movement)." Watt later adds that while the roots of the ICOC could stretch back to the early 1970s, McKean's 1979 takeover of the Lexington congregation was at the very least a major turning point in its history.[52]

Other examples of this interpretive framework abound. For instance, in the first of his agenda-setting "Revolution Through Restoration" articles, Kip McKean claims that:

> When we built these churches, we taught against the unscriptural church government system practiced in the traditional Churches of Christ. They believed that each congregation was independent and totally autonomous from all the others. We showed from the Bible how congregations were connected through their relationships and how evangelists directed other evangelists in the region (field) they influenced. (The word 'autonomy' is not even in the Bible.) We also taught that the lead evangelist worked with, and, for the most part, led and discipled the elders to direct the affairs of a local church (Titus 1:5; 1 Timothy 5:17).[53]

In this selection and in others like it, McKean makes two substantial claims about the early church. The first is that the New Testament sanctions one congregation to have authority over others in matters of doctrine, practice, and discipline. Later in the article, McKean elaborates on this point as he describes his vision of developing Los Angeles into just such a "super church," justifying his decision by appeal to 1 Thessalonians 1:7, and he compares the former leadership role of the Boston congregation to "centers of training [as seen in] the pattern of the book of Acts."[54] The second major line of restorationist theology in the lengthy

McKean quotation is his contention that congregational elders were not the leading figures in the first century churches. Citing Paul's instructions to the young evangelists Timothy and Titus to appoint elders in the churches under their care, McKean implies that elders' authority within the church derives from that of the evangelist, rather than the other way around—a direct challenge to the structure typically found within Churches of Christ.[55]

In making these claims, McKean is not simply describing his views on the early church; he is also taking pains to distinguish between "traditional Churches of Christ" and those who were affiliated with him. He critiques Churches of Christ for failing to disavow congregational polity and restore what he sees as a biblically mandated church hierarchy. By contrast, those with him "showed from the Bible" the need for such connections between congregations and pointed out that "The word 'autonomy' is not even in the Bible"—again illustrating the restorationist impulse within ICOC theology and implying that Churches of Christ had no more fully restored the early church than any other group.

Another powerful example of this recursion toward 1979 is found in the writings of Alvin Jennings, whose edited collection *Introducing the Church of Christ* remains a popular evangelistic tool among conservative mainstream Churches of Christ but whose own personal affinity for the Boston Movement sparked no small amount of controversy.[56] In *How Christianity Grows in the City*, a 1985 work dedicated to "all the saints in Christ Jesus at Boston, Massachusetts," Jennings offers a breathless account of McKean's arrival at the Lexington church.

> And so he came, along with his wife Elena and about ten young people, the first week in June, 1979. He already knew that he could not accomplish anything by his own strength, but trusted that God's power could do more than he could imagine as it would work in him and in the few Christians at Lexington (Eph. 3:20). Kip began to instill his own vision into the hearts of the rest, of how God's power could work through all of them if each one would accept the challenge of teaching and training others to teach in the spirit of 2 Timothy 2:2...[57]

Despite noticeable differences regarding the exact timing of the ICOC's birth, there is nevertheless a general agreement among these and other ICOC authors that the movement's own history contains laudable and, more importantly, imitable figures, leaders whose attempts to restore the early church are themselves worthy of emulation and adoration in the present day.

A DOUBLE RECURSION?

Kip McKean was removed from his position as leader of the ICOC in 2001.[58] But he was not finished with the group yet. In the summer of 2003, McKean was asked to take over the ICOC congregation in Portland, Oregon, where a sizable contingent of members were still receptive to his leadership style. Gradually, he began calling for the ICOC to return to the practices and organizational structures which he believed had made the body successful in the 1990s. He also started inviting others to train under him at the Portland church and began sending out the congregation's bulletin throughout the ICOC. These practices, reminiscent of the Gainesville, Boston, and Los Angeles churches during their respective heydays, paved the way for McKean to proclaim that he was still the leader of "God's Modern Day Movement"—and that believers from each of the Stone-Campbell Movement traditions should and would soon come together under his authority.[59]

By the mid-aughts, however, the ICOC was being pulled in a variety of directions, and only some members heeded McKean's call to action. By contrast, four other notable ICOC figures—Gordon Ferguson, Gregg Marutzky, Al Baird, and Mike Taliaferro—traveled to Texas for the 2004 Abilene Christian University lectureship to discuss recent changes within the group and to begin seeking some sort of rapprochement with mainstream Churches of Christ. Yet McKean did retain a sizable personal following, and in 2006, the leaders of the Central New York Church of Christ asked their members to officially cast their lots with Kip. Later that same year, a group made up of these New York brethren and of members of McKean's Portland congregation planted the Chicago International Christian Church. To borrow the words of one chronicler, "This was in fact the first 'church planting' of what was clearly becoming a new Movement!"[60] McKean also decided to move the headquarters of his new group from Portland to a larger city, ultimately settling on Los Angeles in 2007. Since that time, the City of Angels International Christian Church has served as the leading congregation of the International Christian Church/Sold-Out Discipling Movement and, since 2012, as the headquarters of the International College of Christian Ministries, a training program for ICC leaders and members.[61]

Though little has been written on the International Christian Church/Sold-Out Discipling Movement—the two most important books on the ICOC were published in 2005, a year before Kip McKean's ultimate departure from that group—the ICC is also beginning to manifest its own recursions, ranging from the beginning of McKean's ministry in the 1970s to the movement's own origins in the mid-2000s. To date, only one (borderline hagiographical) work on McKean's life, written by Ron Harding, a close associate of McKean, has addressed the ICC/SODM at any great length. This apologia for the ICC demonstrates a continued commitment to restorationism on multiple levels.

> The primary purposes of this exciting narration are to honor God with the truth and to encourage those who have never had the dream – or perhaps have lost it – to share in Jesus' dream of the "evangelization of all nations in this generation." (1 Timothy 2:3-4) Since we live in an age in which the proliferation of information is often distorted, I have sought to carefully investigate and document with first-hand accounts – including my own – the incredible story of the spread of true Christianity from the 1970's to this very day. Much of this rich history is intertwined with the life of my ***"partner in the Gospel"*** Kip McKean – known as a preacher, missionary, reformer, theologian and humanitarian.

Harding's introduction strongly resembles in style the opening lines of Luke-Acts, with its emphasis on eyewitness evidence and implied skepticism, or at least ambivalence, toward other accounts. Harding even borrows the language of "careful investigation" directly from the New International Version rendition of Luke 1. While the theological implications of mirroring McKean's life story with one of the gospel accounts may strike some readers as unusual, Harding's authorial decision nevertheless reflects a mindset and approach shaped by the writings of the early church. Additionally, Harding writes that his goal is to remind readers of Jesus' supposed vision of worldwide evangelization in one generation. Presumably, there would be no reason to remind readers of this overarching purpose if there was no need for them to restore it in the present day.[62]

Here and elsewhere, Harding implies that "true Christianity" began spreading once again in the 1970s, the decade in which McKean began working as a minister within Churches of Christ. This recursion toward the beginning of McKean's ministry is not the only recursion within ICC theology, however. Elsewhere within *The Chronicles of Modern-Day Christianity*, Harding takes great care to distinguish between mainstream Churches of Christ and the ICOC, emphasizing McKean's desire for the latter to be a "Bible Church" rather than a "New Testament Church." Similarly, he emphasizes the discontinuity between the McKean-era ICOC approach to biblical interpretation ("Silent where the Bible speaks, and speak where the Bible is silent") and that of Churches of Christ ("Speak where the Bible speaks, and be silent where the Bible is silent.")[63]

At still other places within the *Chronicles*, however, the birth of the ICC itself is seen as a paradigm shift away from a damaged, decrepit ICOC and as the beginning of the next stage of God's activity in the present day. "Most in the ICOC in the 90's 'believed' that their leaders were completely unified," Harding argues, "but this was never the case."[64] And after McKean was unjustly forced out of his role by "Kingdom Elders and Kingdom Teachers... [who] were fueled by their feelings of under-appreciation and entitlement," a "leadership vacuum" emerged which led to the "ultimate demise of what was then known and revered as the International Church of Christ... in February 2003."[65] By contrast, Harding writes, "after a valiant three-year effort to bring reform to the crumbling International Churches of Christ (ICOC), the Holy Spirit used Kip, soon joined by other valiant disciples on every continent, to initiate the new Portland/SoldOut Discipling Movement!"[66]

Though there is substantial disagreement between sources, and even within sources, as to when the good old days were, there is equally substantial agreement that those days—whenever they may have been—offer believers useful examples and perhaps even a template for restoration in the present day.

CONCLUSION: EMERGING RECURSIONS

The central claim of this chapter is not that the groups examined above are in any way unique among restorationist fellowships in seeking to restore their respective roots, nor is it that newer "restore points" or "time capsules" (to borrow from the world of personal computing) ever fully replace the early church in the historical ecclesiologies of those fellowships. Yet in practice, they—and almost certainly others—have indeed sought to return present-day Christianity both to the faith of the first Christians *and* to the Christianity of earlier generations of their own specific movements.

Because the Emerging Church Movement is still a very young movement, and because restoration is not necessarily the core facet of the group's theology, its recursive restorationism has not developed as fully as those of the other groups we have covered so far. There are signs, however, that some within the ECM are already thinking critically about how their movement has changed since its inception and, on occasion, lamenting those changes. These steps, tentative as they may be, help us see just how pervasive the recursive tendency is.

One very visible example of a nascent recursive restorationism—which comes with the caveat that the author was no longer part of the ECM at the time of writing—is found in the musings of controversial pastor Mark Driscoll. Driscoll, once a member of the proto-ECM Young Leaders Network, criticized the group for losing sight of its end goal in a 2006 article for the *Criswell Theological Review*: "the original purpose of getting on mission may be overlooked" within ECM circles, he sighs, "because there is little agreement on the message or the mission of the Church."[67] On a related note, Kester Brewin observes in *Signs of Emergence* that "as the emerging church movement ages, there are bound to be those within it who will feel that it has 'denominated' too far from them, and who want to push the boundaries further, while others want to spend time properly maturing in the new ground that has been explored."[68] Ray S. Anderson likewise offered a word of caution in 2006 to those in the movement who, he felt, had become so preoccupied with new technologies and worship forms that they had lost sight of the power of the gospel itself. "I have sensed in some of the more recent literature on the emerging church the taste of new wine rather than the vintage gospel," he argues, equating "new wine" with the "new methods, innovative worship and multimedia approach to presenting the gospel... [that] satisfy the need for stimulation, but... lead to spiritual malnutrition" without the sustenance provided by the good news itself.[69]

Again, it is too early to tell whether the ECM will manifest a full-blown case of recursive restorationism, much less to fully understand the specific character of the recursions that may develop. Nevertheless, the tantalizing hints that we have seem to indicate that future ECM members may seek to imitate first generation figures of their movement because of their perceived ability to balance cultural flexibility with a gospel fixation. If so, they will only be following in the footsteps of countless other Christians, which is, of course, a quite appropriate conclusion to our discussion of recursion.

EPILOGUE
REPETITION

Although the preceding chapter on recursion also functions as this work's conclusion in that it brings the historical narrative up to the present day (or near to it, at least),[1] it is still necessary to offer a few brief thoughts on the broader applicability of historical ecclesiology as a category of analysis and on the seeming omnipresence of restorationism throughout history. While this project has focused on four specific groups which have arisen in the Anglophone world within the last two or so centuries, I do not find them to be categorically different from all other restorationist fellowships. (Indeed, it is likely that if these widely varying groups all share some trait, then that trait is probably inherent to restorationism writ large.) As such, I submit the following remarks to highlight the general prevalence of restorationist thought across time and space, to restate the specific conclusions of each chapter, and to suggest some potentially fruitful areas of research into each aspect of historical ecclesiology outlined in this project.

On the applicability of "historical ecclesiology," or the use of a restorationist group's conception of the early church as a category of analysis, it would be hard to overstate the prevalence of restorationism within religious history. To wit, the theologian and historian Alfred T. DeGroot argues in his 1960 *The Restoration Principle* that "The history of all continuing religions is a record of recurring restoration programs" and that his own "Disciples of Christ represent one in the large number of restoration movements that have arisen in the long career of the church."[2] Given the widespread use of restorationist rhetoric and ideals across time and space, it is my hope that future studies will help illuminate the similarities and the differences of belief across restorationist fellowships, in turn allowing us to further refine our definition of "restorationist" in ways that acknowledge the concept's inherent flexibility without losing sight of the common theological ground occupied by its constituent groups.

On that note, one promising area of inquiry relates to restorationists' views on the content and interpretation of divine revelation. While there is a general consensus among restorationists (as among Christians more broadly) regarding the biblical canon, that consensus is not absolute. One notable exception, of course, is the Church of Jesus Christ of Latter-day Saints, which holds to a much larger canon of inspired works, including, among other texts, the Book of Mormon. Further research along these lines will certainly benefit from the insights of RoseAnn Benson's comparative study of Joseph Smith and Alexander Campbell, as well as of John G. Turner's exploration of how portrayals and perceptions of Jesus have changed throughout the church's history.[3]

That restorationist Christians can define—and have defined—the normative early church in different ways (the ECM "recalibration" being one notable example) should clue us in to the potential uses for historical ecclesiology in other contexts.[4] For instance, we have already referred to works like Jason H. Dormady's *Primitive Revolution* and William Mervin Moorhouse's dissertation on Jacksonian rhetoric which spotlight the presence of restorationist thought in the political sphere. More recent contributions like John Fea's *Believe Me* (particularly its discussion of the "Make America Great Again" campaign slogan) and Craig Fehrman's *Author in Chief* also offer glimpses of this phenomenon, though certainly additional work could and should be done in this vein.[5]

One persistent issue for some restorationist groups seeking to fully replicate the early church experience in the present day is their firm belief that the work of the Holy Spirit has in some way changed or ceased since the first century. This is not the case for all restorationist-leaning churches, however. Randall J. Stephens has noted the deep affinity of Holiness and Pentecostal Christians for restorationist theology and rhetoric. Of the former, he writes that they "relied heavily on the primitivist tradition. They sought a return to what they considered to be the unadorned church of scripture, and dismissed all traditions and creeds they deemed antithetical to this goal."[6] Likewise, of the latter, he contends that many adherents "adopted pentecostalism because it affirmed so much of what they had come to believe about the New Testament church and Christian history."[7] (One might less charitably identify the atomizing tendency toward division among Pentecostal

Christians as another aspect in which they resemble many restorationists.)[8]

Because the desire to return to origins is deeply rooted in restorationism, it is perhaps not so surprising that restorationists have also sometimes sought, purposefully or otherwise, to turn back the clock to the early days of their respective movements, not just to the halcyon days of the early church. Three of our featured groups have already manifested this tendency, but again, they are hardly unique in this regard. In fact, one of the clearest examples of this idealization of origins is found in the history of the Primitive Methodists. DeGroot has elsewhere noted the presence of restorationism in John Wesley's thought,[9] but some within subsequent generations of Methodists would in turn question "if '*primitive* Methodism' had not had 'more of sanctity —holiness of Christian perfection in it than *modern* Methodism?'" With that restoration, they believed, "the society might recover some of its original purity," and the "first step in this direction...was a return to the idea that, even though circuit preachers were specially called to full-time evangelism, they were essentially lay workers in a lay community."[10]

In his seminal 1965 article "'The Restoration Principle': A Critical Analysis," Roy B. Ward (of Churches of Christ) called for the kind of meaningful scholarly investigation which "is certainly appropriate if this principle is to be taken seriously." Such an undertaking, he continued, would require the efforts of experts from many disciplines: "biblical studies, church history in general, American church history in particular, theology and philosophy." Much like Ward's "suggestive problematic essay," this work "is offered... not as the definitive solution" but as an impetus for further research. Many other scholars have already made important contributions in the intervening decades since Ward's call to action. Yet it remains my hope, as an American religious historian, to have contributed to this task in some small way.[11]

NOTES

INTRODUCTION

1. Edwin S. Gaustad, "Editorial: Barbarians and Memory," *Journal of Church and State* 37, no. 1 (Winter 1995): 8–9. I am not the first historian of the Stone-Campbell Movement to note Gaustad's somewhat dismissive attitude toward restorationism. The Catholic historian Richard M. Tristano, writing in 1988, argued that another of Gaustad's works displayed "precisely the wrong approach for an outsider. Gaustad is condescending and insulting when he uses terms such as 'clichés,' 'hackneyed,' 'minutiae,' and 'Pharisaism' to discuss some of the most central tenets of belief associated with the Churches of Christ." See Richard M. Tristano, *The Origins of the Restoration Movement: An Intellectual History* (Atlanta, GA: Glenmary Research Center, 1988), 173.
2. Mark A. Noll, *The Scandal of the Evangelical Mind* (Grand Rapids, MI: Wm. B. Eerdmans Publishing Co., 1994), 158–159. It is worth noting that Noll has been more charitable toward the Stone-Campbell Movement in other writings, including his foreword to William R. Baker, ed., *Evangelicalism and the Stone-Campbell Movement* (Downers Grove, IL: InterVarsity Press, 2002).
3. Seth Perry, "Scripture, Time, and Authority among Early Disciples of Christ," *Church History* 85, no. 4 (December 2016): 764, 777.
4. Even professional historians are hardly immune to errors, whether committed through mindlessness or malfeasance. For not a few examples of each, see David Hackett Fischer, *Historians' Fallacies: Toward a Logic of Historical Thought* (New York: Harper & Row Publishers, Inc., 1970); Jon Wiener, *Historians in Trouble: Plagiarism, Fraud, and Politics in the Ivory Tower* (New York: New Press, 2005); and Nachman Ben-Yehuda and Amalya Oliver-Lumerman, *Fraud and Misconduct in Research: Detection, Investigation, and Organizational Response* (Ann Arbor, MI: University of Michigan Press, 2017).
5. See, for instance, the relevant sections in Leslie R. Galbraith and Heather F. Day, *The Disciples and American Culture: A Bibliography of Works by Disciples of Christ Members, 1866-1984* (Metuchen, NJ: The Scarecrow Press, Inc., 1990); Paul W. Riddle, "An Annotated Bibliography of Articles on Restoration History Published in *Restoration Quarterly* from 1957 to 1983," *Restoration Quarterly* 28, no. 4 (1985-1986): 235–

247; Mark W. Hamilton, "Transition and Continuity: Biblical Scholarship in Today's Churches of Christ," *Stone-Campbell Journal* 9, no. 2 (Fall 2006): 187–203; William R. Baker, Paul J. Kissling, and Tony Springer, "Coming Full Circle: Biblical Scholarship in Christian Churches," *Stone-Campbell Journal* 10, no. 2 (Fall 2007): 165–191; and William R. Baker, "Addendum to 'Coming Full Circle: Biblical Scholarship in Christian Churches,'" *Stone-Campbell Journal* 11, no. 1 (Spring 2008): 93–95.

6. To that end, "Hundreds of thousands of Americans who do not earn their living as history professionals dedicate considerable time, money, and even love to historical pursuits.... our survey would suggest that 20 million Americans pursue historical hobbies and collections." See Roy Rosenzweig and David Thelen, *The Presence of the Past: Popular Uses of History in American Life* (New York: Columbia University Press, 2000), 34.
7. Bill J. Humble, "The Restoration Ideal in the Churches of Christ," in Richard T. Hughes, ed., *The American Quest for the Primitive Church* (Urbana, IL: University of Illinois Press, 1988), 220, lays important groundwork by acknowledging that "Churches of Christ are most indebted to three leaders for their restoration theology," not all of whom were contemporaries: "Thomas and Alexander Campbell in the period between 1800 and 1850, and David Lipscomb during the decades following the Civil War."
8. In particular, see Edward Schillebeeckx, *The Church with a Human Face: A New and Expanded Theology of Ministry*, trans. John Bowden (New York: The Crossroad Publishing Company, 1985).
9. Roger Haight, *Christian Community in History, Volume I: Historical Ecclesiology* (New York: Continuum, 2004), 6.
10. Neil Ormerod, *Re-Visioning the Church: An Experiment in Systematic-Historical Ecclesiology* (Minneapolis, MN: Fortress Press, 2014), 10.
11. Finding membership numbers for these groups is not always straightforward. An article from the BBC, last updated in 2009, claims that for the Christadelphians, "one estimate is that there are about 50,000 members in 120 countries worldwide, 6,500 of them in the USA." (See "Christadelphians," *BBC*, June 25, 2009, https://www.bbc.co.uk/religion/religions/christianity/subdivisions/christadelphians_1.shtml.) For the non-institutional Churches of Christ, the 2015 edition of *Churches of Christ in the United States* (21st Century Christian, 2015) compiled by Carl H. Royster claims 2,918 churches with 163,202 in attendance. And for the International Churches of Christ, "reported membership hit a high of 135,000 in 2002 [but had by 2006] plummeted to less than 89,000—a 34 percent decline." (See Bobby Ross Jr., "Revisiting the Boston movement: ICOC growing again after crisis," *Christian Chronicle*, September 1, 2012,

https://christianchronicle.org/revisiting-the-boston-movement-icoc-growing-again-after-crisis/.)

12. Even the *Handbook of Denominations* is stumped by the task of counting ECM members, listing "Membership: statistics not available" in the entry for Emergent Village. See "Emergent Village" in Frank S. Mead, Samuel S. Hill, and Craig D. Atwood, eds., *Handbook of Denominations in the United States*, 13th ed. (Nashville, TN: Abingdon Press, 2010), 296.
13. Christian unity was one of the main goals, if not the primary motivating force, from the outset of the movement; "Yet precisely how to end Christian division and embrace visible Christian unity became the issue." Many in Stone's camp believed that removing creeds and denominational structures would suffice, though Campbell added "the restoration of the ancient order of things" to that list, which complicated matters considerably. In the long run, the "call to unity often appeared to other Christians as nothing more than a call to join their denomination." For more on the tension between restoration and unity in SCM history, as well as recent efforts taken by movement leaders to mend fences between the various fellowships, see D. Newell Williams, Douglas A. Foster, and Paul M. Blowers, eds., *The Stone-Campbell Movement: A Global History* (St. Louis, MO: Chalice Press, 2013), 367–379.
14. As Richard T. Hughes has observed in his own treatment of the relevant historiography, this early understanding of Churches of Christ as the schismatic sister of the Disciples has been "central to Disciples' historiography" and has appeared in numerous synthetic studies of American religious history. As Hughes also noted, however, historians within Churches of Christ have often seen the history of the Stone-Campbell Movement in a similar light—only with themselves as the faithful trunk and the other groups, especially the Disciples, as the wayward branches. See Richard T. Hughes, *Reviving the Ancient Faith: The Story of Churches of Christ in America* (Grand Rapids, MI: William B. Eerdmans Publishing Company, 1996), 14–15.
15. An important early step away from this self-siloing was Michael W. Casey and Douglas A. Foster, "The Renaissance of Stone-Campbell Studies: An Assessment and New Directions," in *The Stone-Campbell Movement: An International Religious Tradition*, ed. Michael W. Casey and Douglas A. Foster (Knoxville, TN: The University of Tennessee Press, 2002), 1–65.
16. Douglas A. Foster et al, eds., *The Encyclopedia of the Stone-Campbell Movement* (Grand Rapids, MI: Wm. B. Eerdmans Publishing, 2004).
17. D. Newell Williams, Douglas A. Foster, and Paul M. Blowers, eds., *The Stone-Campbell Movement: A Global History* (St. Louis, MO: Chalice Press, 2013).

18. That some of the fellowships on the edges of the Stone-Campbell Movement—specifically, the Christadelphians and the ICOC—are restorationist is not a universally accepted tenet. For instance, historian David Edwin Harrell Jr. has argued that the ICOC was "an aberration that, like the Christadelphians of the nineteenth century, drifted far from restoration moorings and came to have a life of its own." See David Edwin Harrell, Jr., *The Churches of Christ in the Twentieth Century: Homer Hailey's Personal Journey of Faith* (Tuscaloosa, AL: The University of Alabama Press, 2000), 181. I argue here, however, that because members of these groups still seek to restore aspects of the example and precedent of the earliest Christians (no matter how much their descriptions of the early church differ) they are still restorationists.
19. A handful of scholars have begun to highlight the restorationist tendencies of the ECM, identifying the similarities between it and more traditionally restorationist fellowships, such as those of the Stone-Campbell Movement—though more work remains to be done. See, for instance, Elesha Coffman, "Postmodern Campbellites?" *Religion in American History* (blog), June 19, 2014, https://usreligion.blogspot.com/2014/06/postmodern-campbellites.html, which is discussed in greater length in Chapter Three, "Replication."
20. Bryan R. Wilson, *Sects and Society: A Sociological Study of Three Religious Groups in Britain* (London: W. Heinemann, 1961; repr., Westport, CT: Greenwood, 1978).
21. In *Sects and Society*'s section on Christadelphianism, Wilson remains "principally concerned" with the Central Fellowship, the largest subdivision within the Christadelphian tradition. See Wilson, *Sects and Society*, 220.
22. Wilson, *Sects and Society*, 3. Wilson was an important contributor to the systematic development of the "secularization thesis" during the 1960s and 1970s. For more on Wilson and his connection to the thesis, see Hugh McLeod, *Secularisation in Western Europe, 1848-1914* (New York: St. Martin's, 2000), 2–3.
23. Wilson, *Sects and Society*, 3.
24. Wilson, *Sects and Society*, 6–7. Like the later Christadelphians, Miller and his followers were concerned about the trend toward schism within contemporary American Protestantism, seeing "the nation's doctrinal Babel as a telling sign of the times, ample proof of impending judgment for the nation rather than millennial paradise." Rather than splitting off into a separate denomination, at least initially, they remained within their "predominantly Baptist, Methodist, and Presbyterian churches... until the final year before the Great Disappointment." See Ryan Cordell, "'This Flattering Millennium Theory': Denominationalism against

Millennialism in James Fenimore Cooper's *The Crater*," in *Apocalypse and the Millennium in the American Civil War Era*, eds. Ben Wright and Zachary W. Dresser (Baton Rouge: Louisiana State University Press, 2013), 58.

25. Wilson's influence can also be seen in Christadelphians' descriptions of their own past. See, for instance, the reference to Wilson in T.J. Barling, "The World of 1864 and the Household," in *One Hundred Years of The Christadelphian: A Centenary Review of the Magazine and the Community, July, 1864, to July, 1964* (Birmingham: The Christadelphian, 1964), 11.
26. Lippy developed a scholarly interest in Christadelphianism after a chance meeting with a believer while a student at Union Theological Seminary. After realizing that "there was no monograph or article devoted exclusively to explaining and analyzing this group," Lippy took it upon himself to write an MDiv thesis and, later, a monograph doing just that. See Charles H. Lippy, *The Christadelphians in North America* (Lewiston, NY: The Edwin Mellen Press, 1989), iii.
27. Lippy, *The Christadelphians in North America*, 3–4, 6, 13, 20.
28. Wilson, *Sects and Society*, 236.
29. Bryan R. Wilson, "Ever on the watch," review of *The Christadelphians in North America*, by Charles H. Lippy, *Times Literary Supplement*, May 18, 1990, 531.
30. Andrew R. Wilson, *The History of the Christadelphians, 1864-1885: The Emergence of a Denomination* (Australia Square, NSW: Shalom Publications, 1997), i.
31. Wilson, *The History of the Christadelphians*, 65, 32.
32. Wilson, *The History of the Christadelphians*, 2.
33. Wilson, *The History of the Christadelphians*, 258.
34. As Charles H. Lippy has defined it, the question of "resurrectional responsibility" is "whether only those who had been baptized into 'the truth' would be resurrected for judgment or whether those who had been exposed to 'the truth' but refused to accept it and be baptized would also be resurrected for judgment." For more, see Lippy, *The Christadelphians in North America*, 68–73.
35. Wilson, *The History of the Christadelphians*, 179.
36. Harrell, *The Churches of Christ in the Twentieth Century*, xi.
37. John C. Hardin, "Common Cause: B.C. Goodpasture, the *Gospel Advocate*, and Churches of Christ in the Twentieth Century" (PhD diss., Auburn University, 2009), 158; John C. Hardin, "Rock Fights, Quarantines, and Confessionals: B.C. Goodpasture, the *Gospel Advocate*, and Keeping Order in Churches of Christ," in *Recovering the Margins of American Religious History: The Legacy of David Edwin Harrell Jr.*, eds. B. Dwain Waldrep and Scott Billingsley (Tuscaloosa, AL: The University of Alabama Press, 2012), 60–83.

38. James Stephen Wolfgang, "Fundamentalism and the Churches of Christ, 1910-1930" (MA thesis, Vanderbilt University, 1990); James Stephen Wolfgang, "Science and Religion Issues in the American Restoration Movement" (PhD diss., University of Kentucky, 1997).
39. Originally given as a speech, the text of Wolfgang's presentation was later printed across four issues of the *Guardian of Truth*, a periodical associated with non-institutional congregations. The above quotation comes from Steve Wolfgang, "History and Background of the Institutional Controversy (3)," *Guardian of Truth*, May 4, 1989, http://truthmagazine.com/archives/volume33/GOT033130.html. The other three parts can be found at Steve Wolfgang, "Speech Delivered at the Nashville Meeting: History and Background of the Institutional Controversy (1)," *Guardian of Truth*, April 6, 1989, http://www.truthmagazine.-com/speech-delivered-at-the-nashville-meeting-history-and-back-ground-of-the-institutional-controversy-1; Steve Wolfgang, "History and Background of the Institutional Controversy (2)," *Guardian of Truth*, April 20, 1989, https://www.truthmagazine.com/archives/volume33/GOT033115.html; and Steve Wolfgang, "History and Background of the Institutional Institutional Controversy (4)," *Guardian of Truth*, May 18, 1989, http://www.truthmagazine.com/archives/volume33/GOT033136.html.
40. Margie H. Garrett, ed., *Making a Difference: Florida College: The First Fifty Years* (Temple Terrace, FL: Florida College Bookstore, 1996).
41. Ferrell Jenkins, "Please Don't Call Us 'Anti' (An Update on the Non-Institutional Churches of Christ)" (lecture, 55th Anniversary Pepperdine University Bible Lectures, Malibu, CA, May 1, 1998).
42. Larry Hart, "Brief History of a Minor Restorationist Group (The Non-Sunday-School Churches of Christ," *Restoration Quarterly* 22, no. 4 (1979), 212–232; Kent Ellett, "Non-Sunday-School Churches of Christ: Their Origins and Transformation," *Discipliana* 60, no. 2 (Summer 2000), 49–63; Thomas A. Langford, "An insider's view of non-Sunday school Churches of Christ," *Restoration Quarterly* 45, no. 3 (2003), 181–192.
43. Ron Clark, "Pendleton, Franklin, Sommer, and Ketcherside: Mutual Edification in our Roots to Build Up the Body," *Restoration Quarterly* 51, no. 3 (2009), 151. See also Stuart Davis Sockwell, "The 'Pastor System Debate' within the Churches of Christ: An Argumentative Analysis Using a Fields Approach" (MA thesis, University of Alabama, 1990).
44. Kathleen E. Jenkins, "Intimate Diversity: The Presentation of Multiculturalism and Multiracialism in a High-Boundary Religious Movement," *Journal for the Scientific Study of Religion* 42, no. 3 (September 2003): 393–409.

NJ: Rutgers

45. Kathleen E. Jenkins, *Awesome Families: The Promise of Healing Relationships in the International Churches of Christ* (New Brunswick, New Jersey: Rutgers University Press, 2005), 5–6.
46. Jenkins, *Awesome Families*, 6–7.
47. Jenkins, *Awesome Families*, 20.
48. Jenkins, *Awesome Families*, 246–251.
49. C. Foster Stanback, *Into All Nations: A History of the International Churches of Christ* (Newton Upper Falls, MA: Illumination Publishers International, 2005), 12.
50. Stanback, *Into All Nations*, 141–143.
51. Thomas A. Jones, *In Search of a City: An Autobiographical Perspective on a Remarkable but Controversial Movement* (Spring Hill, TN: DPI Books, 2007), 105.
52. Don Vinzant, "Roots of the Modern Discipling Movement," in *The Discipling Dilemma: A Study of the Discipling Movement Among Churches of Christ*, ed. Flavil R. Yeakley Jr. (Nashville, TN: Gospel Advocate Co., 1988), 123.
53. Russell R. Paden, "From the Churches of Christ to the Boston Movement: A Comparative Study" (MA thesis, University of Kansas, 1994), ii–iii.
54. Russell Paden, "The Boston Church of Christ," in *America's Alternative Religions*, ed. Timothy Miller (Albany, NY: State University of New York Press, 1995), 133–140; Russ Paden, "The Boston Church of Christ," in *The Stone-Campbell Movement: An International Religious Tradition*, ed. Michael W. Casey and Douglas A. Foster (Knoxville, TN: The University of Tennessee Press, 2002), 563–573. As the latter is a compilation of previously published works, the material appears to be identical in the two essays.
55. Roger D. Hendricks, "The Development of the International Churches of Christ" (MTS thesis, Christian Theological Seminary, 1997); John F. Wilson, "The International Churches of Christ: A Historical Overview," *Leaven* 18, no. 2 (Second Quarter 2010): 70–73.
56. Gerardo Marti and Gladys Ganiel, *The Deconstructed Church: Understanding Emerging Christianity* (New York: Oxford University Press, 2014), 21. See also Mark Driscoll, "A Pastoral Perspective on the Emergent Church." *Criswell Theological Review* 3, no. 2 (Spring 2006): 87–89.
57. Marti and Ganiel, *The Deconstructed Church*, 25.
58. Steven P. Miller, *The Age of Evangelicalism: America's Born-Again Years* (New York: Oxford University Press, 2014), 148–149.
59. Michael Clawson, "A Brief History of the Emerging Church Movement in the United States," in *Crossing Boundaries, Redefining Faith: Interdisciplinary Perspectives on the Emerging Church Movement*, ed.

Michael Clawson and April Stace (Eugene, OR: Wipf & Stock Publishers, 2016), 17–18.

60. Mathew Guest, "The Emerging Church in Transatlantic Perspective," *Journal for the Scientific Study of Religion* 56, no. 1 (March 2017): 41–42.

1. REVELATION

61. N.T. Wright, *Revelation for Everyone* (Louisville, KY: Westminster John Knox Press, 2011), x.
62. Mitchell Meltzer, *Secular Revelations: The Constitution of the United States and Classic American Literature* (Cambridge, MA: Harvard University Press, 2005), 2.
63. Peter Alward, *Empty Revelations: An Essay on Talk about, and Attitudes toward, Fiction* (Montreal: McGill-Queen's University Press, 2012), 11, 85.
64. Benedek Láng, "Ciphers in Magic: Techniques of Revelation and Concealment," *Magic, Ritual, and Witchcraft* 10, no. 2 (Winter 2015): 125, 136.
65. Michael Taussig, "Viscerality, Faith, and Skepticism: Another Theory of Magic," in *Magic and Modernity: Interfaces of Revelation and Concealment*, eds. Birgit Meyer and Peter Pels (Stanford, CA: Stanford University Press, 2003), 273.
66. Although my subjects often framed this as a simple yes-or-no question (is there a place for these things in the life of the church or not?), in practice, their answers fell along a spectrum or sliding scale, with different individuals and groups reaching varying conclusions about *how much* of this intellectual discourse was useful, appropriate, or beneficial. All ultimately engaged with it to a greater or lesser degree.
67. Because of its quite different intellectual heritage and philosophical underpinnings, I am not engaging with the Emerging Church Movement in this chapter. The next chapter, "Recalibration," which explores how the chronological parameters of the normative "early church" are themselves subject to debate, will focus exclusively on the ECM, however.
68. Sydney E. Ahlstrom, "The Scottish Philosophy and American Theology," *Church History* 24, no. 3 (September 1955): 257.
69. D.F. Kelly, "Scottish Realism," in *Evangelical Dictionary of Theology*, 3rd ed., eds. Daniel J. Treier and Walter A. Elwell (Grand Rapids: Baker Academic, 2017), 790.
70. Luigi Giussani, *American Protestant Theology: A Historical Sketch*, trans. Damian Bacich (Montreal: McGill-Queen's University Press, 2013), 47.

11. *Scottish Common Sense Philosophy: Sources and Origins*, ed. James Fieser, vol. 5, *A Bibliography of Scottish Common Sense Philosophy* (Bristol, England: Thoemmes Press, 2000), vii–viii.
12. S.A. Grave, *The Scottish Philosophy of Common Sense* (New York: Oxford University Press, 1960; repr., Westport, CT: Greenwood Press, Inc., 1973), 4, 12.
13. Ryan Nichols and Gideon Yaffe, "Thomas Reid," in *The Stanford Encyclopedia of Philosophy*, Winter 2016 ed., ed. Edward N. Zalta, https://plato.stanford.edu/archives/win2016/entries/reid/.
14. Peter Novick, *That Noble Dream: The "Objectivity Question" and the American Historical Profession* (New York: Cambridge University Press, 1988), 34.
15. David L. Little, "Inductive Hermeneutics and the Early Restoration Movement," *Stone-Campbell Journal* 3, no. 1 (Spring 2000): 14.
16. Carisse Mickey Berryhill, "Common Sense Philosophy," in *The Encyclopedia of the Stone-Campbell Movement*, ed. Douglas A. Foster, Paul M. Blowers, Anthony L. Dunnavant, and D. Newell Williams (Grand Rapids, MI: William B. Eerdmans Publishing Company, 2004), 231.
17. David H. Warren, "The Men of Glasgow: Influences Upon the Campbells," *Restoration Quarterly* 51, no. 2 (2009): 65–79.
18. Richard T. Hughes, *Reviving the Ancient Faith: The Story of Churches of Christ in America* (Grand Rapids, MI: William B. Eerdmans Publishing Company, 1996), 120.
19. David Edwin Harrell Jr., *The Churches of Christ in the Twentieth Century: Homer Hailey's Personal Journey of Faith* (Tuscaloosa, AL: The University of Alabama Press, 2000), 7.
20. John C. Nugent, "Was Alexander Campbell Enslaved to Scottish Baconianism?" *Stone-Campbell Journal* 12, no. 1 (Spring 2009): 16–17. Additionally, "Campbell rejected the (Lockean) belief that unaided human reasoning can use empirical data to arrive at the idea of God. The witness of Scripture is primary to spiritual ideas, and reason plays a subsequent, supporting role." See Keith Huey, "Campbell, Alexander," in *Biographical Dictionary of Christian Theologians*, eds. Patrick W. Carey and Joseph T. Lienhard (Peabody, MA: Hendrickson Publishers, Inc., 2002), 114.
21. John Thomas, "Bethany College," *Herald of the Kingdom and Age to Come* 1, no. 10 (n.d.), 236–237.
22. John Thomas, "Apostolic Foolishness Better than College Wisdom: or the Restoration of the Kingdom Again to Israel a Reality," *Herald of the Kingdom and Age to Come*, April 1852, 94.
23. The preface of the edition I am using lacks page numbers. See John Thomas, *Eureka: An Exposition of the Apocalypse in Harmony with "the Things of the Kingdom of the Deity and the Name of Jesus Anointed," Volume 1* (West Hoboken, NJ: John Thomas, 1861; repr., West Beach, South

Australia: Logos Publications, n.d.) http://www.antipas.org/pdf_files/eureka_vol_1 _lg.pdf.

24. These quotations also come from the unnumbered preface to Thomas, *Eureka, Vol. 1.*
25. For more, see John Young, "Christadelphian Blueprints for Restoring the Early Church, 1848-1920," *Stone-Campbell Journal* 22, no. 2 (Fall 2019): 165–177.
26. Lippy, *The Christadelphians in North America*, 32–33.
27. Lippy, *The Christadelphians in North America*, 213.
28. Lippy, *The Christadelphians in North America*, 214.
29. Margaret Ann Ross, "Early Camp Meetings in Faulkner County, Arkansas," *Arkansas Historical Quarterly* 10, no. 2 (1951), 165.
30. "Editorial," *Christadelphian eJournal of Biblical Interpretation* 1, no. 1 (Jan. 2007), 2.
31. "Editorial," 2.
32. For a powerful example of the continued influence of the philosophy not covered in this chapter, see the discussion of the non-institutional debate over divorce and remarriage in Harrell, *The Churches of Christ in the Twentieth Century*, 360–366.
33. G.K. Wallace, "Impressions At Bartlesville," *Gospel Guardian*, May 3, 1951, 11b, http://www.wordsfitlyspoken.org/gospel_guardian/v3/ v3n1p11b.html.
34. John T. Lewis, "The Darkest Cloud on Our Horizon," *Bible Banner*, March 1940, http://www.wordsfitlyspoken.org/bible_banner/v2/ v2n8p10-13.html.
35. For more on the life and legacy of Lewis, see, for instance, Chris Cotten, "'The Center and Stronghold of Our Cause in Alabama': Early Stone-Campbell History in Birmingham, Alabama, 1874-1908," *Restoration Quarterly* 59, no. 3 (2017): 141–155.
36. Wallace, "Impressions At Bartlesville," 11b.
37. For more on FC's early history as a distinctly non-institutional school, see Harrell, *The Churches of Christ in the Twentieth Century*, 280–287.
38. James R. Cope, "The Bible And The Curriculum At Florida Christian College," *Gospel Guardian*, May 4, 1950, 4a, http://www.wordsfitlyspoken.org/gospel_guardian/v2/v2n1p4a.html.
39. C.G. "Colly" Caldwell, ed., "Introduction: Laying the Foundation," in *Making a Difference: Florida College: The First Fifty Years*, ed. Margie H. Garrett (Temple Terrace, FL: Florida College Bookstore, 1996), 13.
40. Harrell, *The Churches of Christ in the Twentieth Century*, 283.
41. Clinton D. Hamilton, ed., "Early Years: 1949-1961: New Directions: Controversy and Decision," in *Making a Difference: Florida College: The First Fifty Years*, ed. Margie H. Garrett (Temple Terrace, FL: Florida College Bookstore, 1996), 49.
42. Gloria Baird, "Editorial: Shining Through," *L.A. Story*, March 26, 1995, 2.

43. Marcia Lamb, "'I Love This. I Want This.," *L.A. Story*, March 26, 1995, 3. For a strikingly similar example of a late 1990s-early 2000s Los Angeles church repurposing a club as a space for worship, see the discussion of Erwin McManus's congregation in LaDawn Prieto, "An Urban Mosaic in Shangri-La," in *GenX Religion*, eds. Richard W. Flory and Donald E. Miller (New York: Routledge, 2000), 58.
44. For an extended discussion of the appeal of the ICOC to some women, as well as the church's efforts to attract and retain women converts, see Luann C. Cooley, "Discipling Sisters: How Women Learn the Culture of a Conservative Christian Church" (PhD diss., The University of Georgia, 2006).
45. "March 4, 1995: One Lifechanging Day for Women in L.A.," *L.A. Story*, March 26, 1995, 6.
46. Gloria Baird, "Editorial: Shining Through," *L.A. Story*, March 26, 1995, 2.
47. Elena Garcia-McKean, "Nothing to Hide, But Something to Show.," *L.A. Story*, March 26, 1995, 4.
48. For a sampling of his research work, see A.W. Baird III and D.G. Swanson, "Experimental Investigation of the Ion-Ion Hybrid Resonance," *The Physics of Fluids* 12, no. 9 (September 1969), 1878-1885, as well as A.W. Baird III, "Determination of Electron Density Profiles from Tonks-Dattner Resonance Data in Plasmas," *Journal of Applied Physics* 42, no. 13 (December 1971), 5358–5361.
49. See, for instance, Douglas Leon Hall, "Authoritarian Theology in the Boston Church of Christ: A Short-Circuit of Christianity" (MA thesis, Abilene Christian University, 1991); Richard J. Henegar, "Discipling Churches of Christ: An Assessment of Pre, Peak, and Post Involvement of Former Members Using the Myers-Briggs Type Indicator" (PhD diss., United States International University, 1992); Russell R. Paden, "From the Churches of Christ to the Boston Movement: A Comparative Study" (MA thesis, University of Kansas, 1994); Carl M. Cates, "Cult Rhetoric: A Genre of Manipulative Speech" (PhD diss., Florida State University, 1994); and Patrick Y. Zukeran, "A Critique of the International Church of Christ" (ThM thesis, Dallas Theological Seminary, 1996).
50. Douglas Anderson Jacoby, "Equipping the Members: Organizing an Effective Congregational Teaching Day and Follow-On Program" (DMin project, Drew University, 1999), unnumbered acknowledgements page; G. Steve Kinnard, "New Wineskins: Formation of a Ministry of Multimedia Education Integrating the Bible, Geography, and Archaeology" (DMin project, Drew University, 1999), 9.
51. James Lappeman, "Factors Influencing The International Church of Christ's Decision Not To Require Formal Theological Training For Its

Ministers From 1979-2002" (MA thesis, University of Cape Town, 2014), 58.

52. Lappeman, "Factors Influencing The International Church of Christ's Decision," 60.
53. Lappeman, "Factors Influencing The International Church of Christ's Decision," 60. Ferguson writes in "Progressive Revelation: Part III(B): Specific Examples Explained," *Boston Bulletin*, May 22, 1988, that "My own training in a Preacher's School and a Graduate School, both sponsored by the churches of Christ, left me woefully inadequate in my preparation for ministry. Without question, the discipling approach practiced by Boston and similar congregations is the biblical way to do it!"
54. Lappeman, "Factors Influencing The International Church of Christ's Decision," 60–61.
55. Ronald C. Harding Jr., *The Chronicles of Modern-Day Christianity: The Evangelization of the Nations in This Generation* (Columbia, SC: SoldOut Press International, 2018), 27. Harding also notes on p. 30 that McKean took a year of Greek while at UF which, he asserts, was "later of great value in Kip's in-depth, scholarly Bible studies."
56. Harding Jr., *The Chronicles of Modern-Day Christianity*, 30.
57. Harding Jr., *The Chronicles of Modern-Day Christianity*, 30.
58. Harding Jr., *The Chronicles of Modern-Day Christianity*, 40. The adjective "Mainline" was often used by ICOC members as a pejorative to distinguish the older, declining Churches of Christ fellowship from its younger, more energetic counterpart.
59. Harding Jr., *The Chronicles of Modern-Day Christianity*, 130.
60. Harding Jr., *The Chronicles of Modern-Day Christianity*, 126. A former member of the group has strongly criticized this maneuver, arguing that it was only possible because the school had been exempted from accreditation by the state of California. See "The International College of Christian Ministry (ICCM)," *ExICC*, March 6, 2014, https://www.exicc.org/2014/03/international-college-christian-ministry- iccm.html.
61. Harding Jr., *The Chronicles of Modern-Day Christianity*, 172–174.

2. RECALIBRATION

1. Stuart Chinn, "Institutional Recalibration and Judicial Delimitation," *Law & Social Inquiry* 37, no. 3 (Summer 2012): 536.
2. Ra Mason, *Japan's Relations with North Korea and the Recalibration of Risk* (New York: Routledge, 2014), 4.

3. Carlo Graziani et al, "Probabilistic Recalibration of Forecasts" (working paper, 2019), 3. http://arxiv.org/abs/1904.02855
4. For a useful introduction to scholarship on one Christian fellowship which opts for this particular descriptor, see John G. Crowley, "'Written that Ye May Believe': Primitive Baptist Historiography," in *Through a Glass Darkly: Contested Notions of Baptist Identity*, ed. Keith Harper (Tuscaloosa, AL: University of Alabama Press, 2012), 205–227.
5. Alfred T. DeGroot, *The Restoration Principle* (St. Louis, MO: The Bethany Press, 1960), 20.
6. Maurice Halbwachs, *On Collective Memory*, ed. and trans. Lewis A. Coser (Chicago: University of Chicago Press, 1992), 40.
7. And unconsciously, as shown in the later chapter on recursion.
8. Jason H. Dormady, *Primitive Revolution: Restorationist Religion and the Idea of the Mexican Revolution, 1940-1968* (Albuquerque, NM: University of New Mexico Press, 2011), 3.
9. William Mervin Moorhouse, "The Restoration Movement: The Rhetoric of Jacksonian Restorationism in a Frontier Religion" (PhD diss., Indiana University, 1968), 10. One might also notice some similarities in John Fea's discussion of Donald Trump's fascination with Andrew Jackson. See John Fea, *Believe Me: The Evangelical Road to Donald Trump* (Grand Rapids, MI: William B. Eerdmans Publishing Company, 2018), 166–171.
10. Though it focuses more on ECM self-appraisals rather than on scholarly treatments of the movement, Jason Fikes, "Emerging Historiography: How Church Leaders Are Looking at the Past and Shaping What Is to Come," *Stone-Campbell Journal* 14, no. 2 (Fall 2011): 207–218, concisely provides a useful introduction to many key ECM and ECM-adjacent works.
11. Michael Clawson, in "A Brief History of the Emerging Church Move-ment in the United States," in *Crossing Boundaries, Redefining Faith: Interdisciplinary Perspectives on the Emerging Church Movement*, eds. Michael Clawson and April Stace (Eugene, OR: Wipf & Stock Publishers, 2016), 18, finds important precedents in the countercultural approach of the Jesus People of the 1960s and 1970s. He notes that they "did not simply disappear. Rather, as they matured, got jobs, and started families, they increasingly settled into more mainstream religious settings" and "set the stage for the Emerging Church Movement a generation later."
12. Gerardo Marti and Gladys Ganiel, *The Deconstructed Church: Understanding Emerging Christianity* (New York: Oxford University Press, 2014), 21.
13. Marti and Ganiel, *The Deconstructed Church*, 22.
14. The popular and provocative pastor Mark Driscoll, who was involved with YLN early on, largely confirms this interpretation, though he

argues that several other issues played a role in the group's demise as well. One rather banal contributing factor was the inherent logistical difficulty of physically bringing together church planters who, given the nature of their work, generally needed to be at their churches on the weekends. See Mark Driscoll, "A Pastoral Perspective on the Emergent Church," *Criswell Theological Review* 3, no. 2 (Spring 2006): 89.

15. Clawson, "A Brief History," 35. The *Handbook of Denominations* concisely describes Emergent Village as "not a denomination. Rather it is a network of Christians seeking to find authentic expressions of the gospel in the twenty-first century." See "Emergent Village" in Frank S. Mead, Samuel S. Hill, and Craig D. Atwood, eds., *Handbook of Denominations in the United States*, 13th ed. (Nashville, TN: Abingdon Press, 2010), 296.
16. Brian D. McLaren, *A New Kind of Christian: A Tale of Two Friends on a Spiritual Journey* (San Francisco: Jossey-Bass, 2001).
17. Rob Bell, *Velvet Elvis: Repainting the Christian Faith* (Grand Rapids, MI: Zondervan, 2005).
18. Not to be confused with the similarly named Mars Hill Church in Seattle, Washington, formerly pastored by Mark Driscoll.
19. Clawson, "A Brief History," 36; Andy Crouch, "The Emergent Mystique," *Christianity Today*, November 2004, 38.
20. Phyllis Tickle, *Emergence Christianity: What It Is, Where It Is Going, and Why It Matters* (Grand Rapids, MI: Baker Books, 2012), 105. Marti and Ganiel, in *Deconstructed Church*, 21, also refer to the writings of Doug Gay, who pushes the overseas ECM story back to "Low Church Protestantism (LCM), the ecumenical movement, and the loosening of denominational boundaries after Vatican II.". For more on the ECM in its non-American contexts, see Mathew Guest, "The Emerging Church in Transatlantic Perspective," *Journal for the Scientific Study of Religion* 56, no. 1 (March 2017): 41–51.
21. For a representative selection from this literature, see Barry Dean Baker, "A Critical Analysis of the Theory and Practice of Preaching in the Emerging Church Movement" (PhD diss., Mid-America Baptist Theological Seminary, 2006); John Bolt, "An Emerging Critique of the Postmodern, Evangelical Church: A Review Essay," *Calvin Theological Journal* 41, no. 2 (November 2006): 205–221; Kevin DeYoung and Ted Kluck, *Why We're Not Emergent (By Two Guys Who Should Be)* (Chicago: Moody Publishers, 2008); John Alan Duncan, "A Critical Analysis of Preaching in the Emerging Church" (PhD diss., Southern Baptist Theological Seminary, 2011); John S. Hammett, "An Ecclesiological Assessment of the Emerging Church," *Criswell Theological Review* 3, no. 2 (Spring 2006): 29–49; Woo Joon Kim, "An Evangelical Critique of the Emergent Church's Hermeneutics and Its Effects on Theology, Message, and Method of

Evangelism" (PhD diss., Southwestern Baptist Theological Seminary, 2012); and Larry D. Pettegrew, "Evangelicalism, Paradigms, and the Emerging Church," *The Master's Seminary Journal* 17, no. 2 (Fall 2006): 159–175.

22. For instance, Richard L. Mayhue, "The Emerging Church: Generous Orthodoxy or General Obfuscation?" *The Master's Seminary Journal* 17, no. 2 (Fall 2006): 195. Though Mayhue does not specifically mention the ECM affinity for "ancient-future" or "vintage" faith, his critique seems to have the concept in view.
23. Rob Bell, *Love Wins: A Book About Heaven, Hell, and the Fate of Every Person Who Ever Lived* (New York: HarperOne, 2011). Bell continued this line of inquiry in *The Love Wins Companion: A Study Guide for Those Who Want to Go Deeper*, ed. David Vanderveen (New York: HarperOne, 2011), that same year.
24. Francis Chan and Preston Sprinkle, *Erasing Hell: What God Said About Eternity, and the Things We've Made Up* (Colorado Springs, CO: David C. Cook, 2011); Mark Galli, *God Wins: Heaven, Hell, and Why the Good News is Better than* Love Wins (Carol Stream, IL: Tyndale House Publishers, Inc., 2011).
25. Donald Miller, *Blue Like Jazz: Nonreligious Thoughts on Christian Spirituality*, ltd. ed. (Nashville, TN: Thomas Nelson, 2009). Miller followed up the initial publication of *Blue Like Jazz* with the spinoff *Jazz Notes: Improvisations on* Blue Like Jazz (Nashville, TN: Thomas Nelson, 2008). He has since launched the *StoryBrand* podcast and pivoted into marketing consulting, as evidenced by his most recent book, *Building a StoryBrand: Clarify Your Message So Customers Will Listen* (New York: HarperCollins Leadership, 2017).
26. Donald Miller, *Scary Close: Dropping the Act and Finding True Intimacy* (Nashville, TN: Nelson Books, 2014), 146–147. Elsewhere in the same work, Miller pushed back somewhat on the notion that he had ever been part of a larger movement, writing that "Suddenly I was being lumped in with liberal theologians I'd never heard of. They were convinced we were all friends, meeting in caves to cook up conspiracies." See Miller, *Scary Close*, 121.
27. "About," Wild Goose Festival, accessed December 16, 2019, http://wildgoosefestival.org/about-2016/. For a helpful explanation of the connection, see Philip Kosloski, "How the wild goose became a symbol of vigilance and the Holy Spirit," *Aleteia*, October 2, 2017, https://aleteia.org/2017/10/02/how-the-wild-goose-became-a-symbol-of-vigilance-and-the-holy-spirit/.
28. Phyllis Tickle, who argues that a current "Great Emergence" will ultimately prove as monumental to Christianity as the "Great Reformation"

or the "Great Schism," straightforwardly acknowledges that "the truth, in fact, is that nobody is exactly sure who should and should not be labeled as an 'emergent' or 'emerging.' There is, instead, a spectrum or kind of sliding scale..." See Phyllis Tickle, *The Great Emergence: How Christianity is Changing and Why* (Grand Rapids, MI: Baker Books, 2008), 139.

29. Marti and Ganiel acknowledge problems with the term but nevertheless use it because "the activities of Emerging Christians resemble those of social activists in other social movements. We also think the term 'movement' captures the fluidity and dynamism of emerging congregations." See Marti and Ganiel, *Deconstructed Church*, 6.
30. Scot McKnight, "Five Streams of the Emerging Church: Key elements of the most controversial and misunderstood movement in the church today," *Christianity Today*, February 2007, 36.
31. To this end, the ECM is perhaps best thought of as a vanguard for a larger Christian reckoning with postmodernism. For a brief introduction to that larger conversation, see B.E. Benson, "Postmodernism," in *Evangelical Dictionary of Theology*, 3rd ed., eds. Daniel J. Treier and Walter A. Elwell (Grand Rapids, MI: Baker Academic, 2017): 685–689.
32. McKnight, "Five Streams," 36–39. Two scholars of the ECM have confirmed this last point, finding that even though the movement exhibits diversity in many ways, "compared to other clergy in this sample, the average emergent clergyperson is more liberal in his or her theological political beliefs." See Ryan P. Burge and Paul A. Djupe, "Truly Inclusive or Uniformly Liberal? An Analysis of the Politics of the Emerging Church," *Journal for the Scientific Study of Religion* 53, no. 3 (Sep-tember 2014): 649.
33. For more on Rushdoony's movement and its place in the broader evangelical world, see Steven P. Miller, *The Age of Evangelicalism: America's Born-Again Years* (New York: Oxford University Press, 2014), 142.
34. Driscoll, "Pastoral Perspective," 89–90.
35. Marti and Ganiel, *Deconstructed Church*, 11–21.
36. Marti and Ganiel, *Deconstructed Church*, 13.
37. Marti and Ganiel, *Deconstructed Church*, 14.
38. Marti and Ganiel, *Deconstructed Church*, 19. For one of the most well-known examples of this kind of community, see Shane Claiborne, *The Irresistible Revolution: Living as an Ordinary Radical* (Grand Rapids, MI: Zondervan, 2006).
39. Miller, *The Age of Evangelicalism*, 148–149.
40. J.R. Franke, "Emergent Christianity," in *Evangelical Dictionary of Theology*, 3rd ed., eds. Daniel J. Treier and Walter A. Elwell (Grand Rapids, MI: Baker Academic, 2017), 270.

41. James K.A. Smith, *Who's Afraid of Postmodernism? Taking Derrida, Lyotard, and Foucault to Church* (Grand Rapids, MI: Baker Academic, 2006), 130.
42. Again, to summarize the discussion from my introduction, not all history is good history, but that doesn't mean it isn't history.
43. Other notable theologians who have influenced the movement, particularly with regards to the nature of the church and the Kingdom of God, include Dallas Willard, NT Wright, and John Howard Yoder, as Michael Clawson has noted. See Clawson, "Brief History," 23. Joshua M. Moritz has elsewhere noted that "many Emerging communities have been described as 'ancient-future churches." See Joshua M. Moritz, "Beyond Strategy, Towards the Kingdom of God," *Dialog: A Journal of Theology* 41, no. 1 (Spring 2008): 32.
44. Robert E. Webber, *Evangelicals on the Canterbury Trail: Why Evangelicals Are Attracted to the Liturgical Church* (Waco, TX: Word Books, 1985), 167. On a related note, Webber, a prolific author, also identified a growing confluence among some Catholics and Protestants as to the church's role in the broader world. See Robert E. Webber, *The Church in the World: Opposition, Tension, or Transformation?* (Grand Rapids, MI: Academie Books, 1986).
45. Robert Webber, *Ancient-Future Faith: Rethinking Evangelicalism for a Postmodern World* (Grand Rapids, MI: Baker Books, 1999), 80.
46. Webber, *Ancient-Future Faith*, 91.
47. Scott Bader-Saye, "The Emergent Matrix: A New Kind of Church?" *Christian Century*, November 30, 2004, 21.
48. Doug Pagitt, *Church Re-Imagined: The Spiritual Formation of People in Communities of Faith* (Grand Rapids, MI: Zondervan, 2005), 74.
49. Patrick Malloy, "Rick Warren Meets Gregory Dix: The Liturgical Movement Comes Knocking at the Megachurch Door." *Anglican Theological Review* 92, no. 3 (Summer 2010): 449.
50. Dan Kimball, *The Emerging Church: Vintage Christianity for New Generations* (Grand Rapids, MI: Zondervan, 2003), 223.
51. Dan Kimball, *Emerging Worship: Creating New Worship Gatherings for Emerging Generations* (Grand Rapids, MI: Zondervan, 2004), 83.
52. Ray S. Anderson, *An Emergent Theology for Emerging Churches* (Downers Grove, IL: IVP Books, 2006), 11.
53. Anderson, *Emergent Theology*, 13.
54. Anderson, *Emergent Theology*, 85–86.
55. Karen Theresa Wyble, "Telling Stories: Applying Feminist Writing Strategies to 'Emerging Church' Theologies" (PhD thesis, Pennsylvania State University, 2006), 31.
56. Kimball, *The Emerging Church*, 14.
57. Bell, *Love Wins*, x–xi.

58. McLaren, *A Generous Orthodoxy*, 322.
59. Phyllis Tickle, *The Great Emergence: How Christianity is Changing and Why* (Grand Rapids, MI: Baker Books, 2008), 16.
60. Kate D. Simcox, "Performing Postmodern Christian: Communication in the Emerging Church and the Renegotiation of Divine Knowledge" (PhD diss., Bowling Green State University, 2005), 150.
61. Karyn L. Wiseman, "Grace Space: The Creation of Worship Space for the Postmodern/Emerging Church" (PhD diss., Drew University, 2006), 102.
62. Scott R. Burson, *Brian McLaren in Focus: A New Kind of Apologetics* (Abilene, TX: Abilene Christian University Press, 2016), 41.
63. Marti and Ganiel (*Deconstructed Church*, 94) write of ECM members that "For them, modernists conceive of truth as a set of objective propositions about the world as it really is." Conversely, "For Emerging Christians, what is more important than adjudicating between competing 'truth claims' is discovering truth through stories and lived experiences."
64. Carson, *Becoming Conversant with the Emerging Church*, 55.
65. Rick Warren, in Kimball, *The Emerging Church*, 134.
66. William R. Baker, "The Emerging Church: A Brief History and Helpful Resources," *Christian Standard*, November 23, 2008, *NewsBank*. https://in-foweb.newsbank.com/apps/news/document-view?p=WORLD-NEWS NEWS&docref=news/154B4FE99DCE5B18; William R. Baker, "The Emerging Church and the Stone-Campbell Movement: Some Striking Similarities (Part 1)," *Christian Standard*, November 23, 2008, *NewsBank*. https://infoweb.newsbank.com/apps/news/document-view?p=WORLD-NEWS&docref=news/154B4FE98CFF6868; William R. Baker, "The Emerging Church and the Stone-Campbell Movement: Some Striking Similarities (Part 2)," *Christian Standard*, November 30, 2008, *NewsBank*. https://infoweb.newsbank.com/ apps/news/document-view?p=WORLD-NEWS&docref=news/154B4FE9DDDE7430.
67. Graham Bates, "Removing the Bridge Keeper: Comparing the Pioneer Restoration Movement to the Pioneer Emerging Church Movement" (unpublished manuscript, last modified July 4, 2014), Microsoft Word file, 3–4.
68. Elesha Coffman, "Postmodern Campbellites?" *Religion in American History* (blog), June 19, 2014, https://usreligion.blogspot.com/2014/06/post-modern-campbellites.html; Gerardo Marti and Gladys Ganiel, *The Deconstructed Church: Understanding Emerging Christianity*: Oxford University Press, 2014).
69. Kimball, *The Emerging Church*, 49.
70. Kimball, *Emerging Worship*, 196.

71. Eddie Gibbs and Ryan K. Bolger, *Emerging Churches: Creating Christian Community in Postmodern Cultures* (Grand Rapids, MI: Baker Academic, 2005), 11.
72. Brian D. McLaren, *Everything Must Change: Jesus, Global Crises, and a Revolution of Hope* (Nashville, TN: Thomas Nelson, 2007), 3.
73. Brian D. McLaren, *A Generous Orthodoxy: Why I am a Missional, Evangelical, Post/Protestant, Liberal/Conservative, Mystical/Poetic, Biblical, Charismatic/Contemplative, Fundamentalist/Calvinist, Anabaptist/Anglican, Methodist, Catholic, Green, Incarnational, Depressed-Yet-Hopeful, Emergent, Unfinished Christian*, exp. ed. (Grand Rapids, MI: Zondervan, 2005), 141.
74. Nadia Bolz-Weber, *Pastrix: The Cranky, Beautiful Faith of a Sinner & Saint* (New York: Jericho Books, 2013), 26.
75. James S. Bielo, *Emerging Evangelicals: Faith, Modernity, and the Desire for Authenticity* (New York: New York University Press, 2011), 15.
76. Brian D. McLaren, *The Secret Message of Jesus: Uncovering the Truth That Could Change Everything* (Nashville, TN: Thomas Nelson, Inc., 2006), 78.
77. Bell, *Love Wins*, 107–109.
78. Rob Bell, *What Is the Bible? How an Ancient Library of Poems, Letters, and Stories Can Transform the Way You Think and Feel About Everything* (New York: HarperOne, 2017), 131.
79. Bell, *Velvet Elvis*, 12.
80. Nadia Bolz-Weber, *Accidental Saints: Finding God in All the Wrong People* (New York: Convergent Books, 2015), 140.
81. Sally Morgenthaler, in Kimball, *Emerging Worship*, vi.
82. Kimball, *Emerging Worship*, 78.
83. Kimball, *The Emerging Church*, 138.
84. Brad Harper and Paul Louis Metzger, *Exploring Ecclesiology: An Evangelical and Ecumenical Introduction* (Grand Rapids, MI: Brazos Press, 2009), 234.
85. Leonard Sweet, *The Gospel According to Starbucks: Living with a Grande Passion* (Colorado Springs, CO: WaterBrook Press, 2007), xi.
86. Sweet, *The Gospel According to Starbucks*, 55–56.

3. REPLICATION

87. Philip Mirowski, *The Effortless Economy of Science?* (Durham, NC: Duke University Press, 2004), 216.
88. Philip Mirowski, *Science-Mart: Privatizing American Science* (Cambridge, MA: Harvard University Press, 2011), 295. Mirowski has written at length about this difficulty elsewhere, noting, for instance, that “No one can

achieve the same spacetime coordinate, the same apparatus, the same path of inquiry, and so forth...." See Mirowski, *Effortless Economy*, 217.

3. Sophie K. Piper et al., "Exact replication: Foundation of science or game of chance?" *PLoS Biology* 17, no. 4 (2019), 7.
4. John P.A. Ioannidis, "Why Most Published Research Findings Are False," *PLoS Medicine* 2, no. 8 (August 2005), 696.
5. Ed Yong, "Psychology's Replication Crisis Is Running Out of Excuses," *Atlantic*, November 19, 2018, https://www.theatlantic.com/science/archive/2018/11/psychologys-replication-crisis-real/576223/; Bryan Resnick, "More social science studies just failed to replicate. Here's why this is good." *Vox*, August 27, 2018, https://www.vox.com/science-and-health/2018/8/27/17761466/psychology-replication-crisis-nature-social-science; Christie Aschwanden, "Psychology's Replication Crisis Has Made The Field Better," *FiveThirtyEight*, December 6, 2018, https://fivethirtyeight.com/features/psychologys-replication-crisis-has-made-the-field-better/.
6. This capacity is sometimes described as the ability to completely and totally restore; sometimes, to restore to a satisfactory if incomplete degree; and sometimes, to satisfactorily participate in an ongoing process that by definition can never be finished. Despite the variations between these definitions, there is a shared assumption that Christians have both the obligation and ability to meet whichever demand is thought to be incumbent upon them.
7. Ron Abel, *"Let Her be Covered...": The Hats of Christadelphian Sisters: A Biblical Consideration*. Vernon, British Columbia: Wayside Press Ltd., n.d. http://christadelphianbooks.org/books.html.
8. Al Diestelkamp, "The Unfinished Work of Restoration," *Think On These Things*, April-May-June 2001, 1.
9. As one scholar has written, "the idealized Bible can be singular and unchanging in its abstractness, but material bibles are subject to the historicizing and diversifying effects of, among other things, collation, translation, editing, and publishing. See Perry, "Scripture, Time, and Authority among Early Disciples of Christ," 764.
10. J. Early Arceneaux, "Do We Have What The Apostles Wrote?" *Gospel Guardian*, May 5, 1949, 4, http://www.wordsfitlyspoken.org/gospel_guardian/v1/v1n1p4.html.
11. For more on these divisions over Christadelphian theological particulars, see Wilson, *Sects and Society*, 242–255.
12. The edition of the Ecclesial Guide used here does not have page numbers so section numbers are used to indicate where each quotation can be found in the Guide. See Robert Roberts, *The Truth in the Nineteenth Century: or the Lessons of Thirty Years' Experience Presented in the*

Form of a Guide to the Formation and Conduct of Ecclesias, in the Characteristic Circumstances of an Age when the Truth as Apostolically Delivered has been Revived in the Ways of Divine Providence, Without the Co-Operation and Living Guidance of the Holy Spirit as Enjoyed in the Apostolic Age (Birmingham: Robert Roberts, 1883) http://www.antipas.org/pdf_files/e_g_1883.pdf.

13. "Ecclesial Guide," section 4, "Revival of the Apostolic Faith."
14. "Ecclesial Guide," section 14, "Absence of the Spirit's Appointments."
15. "Ecclesial Guide," section 4, "Revival of the Apostolic Faith."
16. "Ecclesial Guide," section 16, "Mutual Consent the Basis of Order."
17. The Christadelphians are not alone among SCM fellowships in this view. One scholar has noted that "The *verbal-restrictive* or 'word only' theory was widely held in Churches of Christ in the twentieth century, though a variety of understandings could be seen, including the nonmiraculous personal indwelling of the Spirit in the Christian." See Byron C. Lambert, "Holy Spirit, Doctrine of the," in *The Encyclopedia of the Stone-Campbell Movement*, 403.
18. For more on this Wallace brother, see Noble Patterson and Terry J. Gardner, eds., *Foy E. Wallace, Jr.: Soldier of the Cross* (Fort Worth, TX: Wallace Memorial Fund, 1999), as well as Terry J. Gardner, "Wallace, Foy Esco [Foy E. Wallace, Jr.] (1896-1979)," in *The Encyclopedia of the Stone-Campbell Movement*, 767–768.
19. Foy E. Wallace, Jr., "The Infidelity of God's People," *Bible Banner*, May 1941, 2, http://www.wordsfitlyspoken.org/bible_banner/v3/v3n10p2-3.html.
20. Wallace, Jr., "The Infidelity of God's People," 2.
21. Cled E. Wallace, "The Right Brand," *Gospel Guardian*, May 5, 1949, 7, http://www.wordsfitlyspoken.org/gospel_guardian/v1/v1n1p1,7b.html. For more on this Wallace brother, see Terry J. Gardner, "Wallace, Cled Eugene 'Cleddie' (1892-1962)," in *The Encyclopedia of the Stone-Campbell Movement*, 766–767.
22. Gordon Ferguson, "Progressive Revelation Part I: The Concept Explained," *Boston Bulletin*, May 1, 1988.
23. Gordon Ferguson, "Progressive Revelation Part V: Brotherhood Unity and World Evangelism," *Boston Bulletin*, June 5, 1988.
24. Ferguson, "Progressive Revelation Part I."
25. Al Baird, "Authority and Submission Part III," *Boston Bulletin*, September 20, 1987.
26. Al Baird, "Editorial: Happy 40th Birthday, Kip," *L.A. Story*, May 1994.
27. Sarah Dannemiller, "Power in Submission: An Analysis of Gender Roles within the Boston Church of Christ, 1979-1989" (unpublished manuscript, last modified April 28, 2015), Microsoft Word file, 4, 17.
28. Sheila Jones, "Greeting One Another," in *Glory in the Church: Powerful Readings Exploring the Eternal Plan for the Family of God*, eds. Thomas

Jones and Sheila Jones (Woburn, MA: Discipleship Publications International, 1996), 98.

29. Terrie Fontenot, "Spurring One Another On," in Jones and Jones, *Glory in the Church*, 123.
30. Al Baird, "Authority and Submission Part II," September 13, 1987. As mentioned in the previous chapter, Baird had himself left a promising career in physics (in which he had earned a doctorate from the University of Texas) to enter the ministry.
31. Kathleen E. Jenkins, "Intimate Diversity: The Presentation of Multiculturalism and Multiracialism in a High-Boundary Religious Movement," *Journal for the Scientific Study of Religion* 42, no. 3 (September 2003), 393–409. Jenkins would address these and similar themes at greater length in her previously cited book, *Awesome Families*, which was published two years later.
32. Gregory C. Stanczak, "Strategic ethnicity: The construction of multiracial/multi-ethnic religious community," *Ethnic and Racial Studies* 29, no. 5 (September 2006), 856–881.
33. Joseph Eugene Yi, "God and Karate in the Southside: American Culture and Civic Participation in a Global Era, Volume One" (PhD diss., The University of Chicago, 2004), vii.
34. Scott Green, "Public Preaching and Teaching in the Early Church, Part III: Public Preaching and Teaching in the Book of Acts," *Boston Bulletin*, November 9, 1986.
35. Scott Green, "Public Preaching and Teaching in the Early Church, Part II: The Public Teaching Strategy of Jesus," *Boston Bulletin*, November 2, 1986.
36. Scott Green, "Public Preaching and Teaching in the Early Church, Part VII: The Public Preaching Legacy of the New Testament," *Boston Bulletin*, December 7, 1986.
37. Jaime L. DeAnda, "A Church of Many Nations," *Boston Bulletin*, January 18, 1987.
38. Al Baird, "Editorial: The Family Grows," *L.A. Story*, October 8, 1995, 2.
39. Mike Taliaferro, "Cry Freedom in South Africa," *L.A. Story*, January 1994, 3. Taliaferro has also sought to root other ICOC practices in the practices and teachings of the early church: "Since the New Testament calls us to study the Old Testament, this, too, must be taught to the new Christian.... While we have made some progress in our restoration of biblical one-on-one discipling, we still have many Christians who are fed far too much junk food instead of solid food from the word of God." Mike Taliaferro, *The Lion Never Sleeps: Preparing Those You Love for Satan's Attacks* (Spring, TX: Illumination Publishers, 2014), 27.
40. Al Baird, "Editorial: Do the Right Thing," *L.A. Story*, April 1999, 2.

41. "'That They May Be One...': John 17:11," *L.A. Story*, April 1999, 5.

4. RECURSION

1. Examples from these disciplines include, for instance, Tom Roeper and Margaret Speas, eds., *Recursion: Complexity in Cognition* (Cham, Switzerland: Springer International Publishing Switzerland, 2014) and Piergiorgio Odifreddi, *Classical Recursion Theory: The Theory of Functions and Sets of Natural Numbers* (New York: Elsevier Science Publishing Company, Inc., 1989).
2. Douglas Hofstadter, *Gödel, Escher, Bach: An Eternal Golden Braid*. Twentieth anniversary ed. (New York: Basic Books, 1999), 127. For more on recursion in a theological context, see chapter 4 of John Young, *Redrawing the Blueprints for the Early Church: Historical Ecclesiology in and around the Stone-Campbell Movement* **(Florence, AL: HCU Press, 2021).**
3. Gary Holloway, *Saints, Demons, and Asses: Southern Preacher Anecdotes* (Bloomington, IN: Indiana University Press, 1989), 13.
4. Similarly, Douglas A. Foster observed in the mid-1990s, "Nostalgia has definitely set in among some of us. Many long for something that used to be, for better days, now seen as slipping away, when 'we stood for something.'" See Douglas A. Foster, *Will the Cycle Be Unbroken? Churches of Christ Face the 21st Century* (Abilene, TX: ACU Press, 1994), xi.
5. Earl Irvin West, *The Search for the Ancient Order*, vol. 2: *A History of the Restoration Movement, 1866-1906* (Indianapolis, IN: Religious Book Service, 1950), xii.
6. Kerrie Handasyde, "Pioneering Leadership: Historical Myth-Making, Absence, and Identity in the Churches of Christ in Victoria," *Journal of Religious History* 41, no. 2 (June 2017): 249. See also Kerrie Handasyde, "Transforming History: The Origins of the Stone-Campbell Movement in Victoria, Australia," *Stone-Campbell Journal* 17, no. 1 (Spring 2014): 3–18.
7. Seth Perry, "Scripture, Time, and Authority among Early Disciples of Christ," 777.
8. Lippy, *The Christadelphians in North America*, 78 n.40.
9. Frank G. Jannaway, *Christadelphian Answers on All Kinds of Difficulties, Objections, Arguments, and Questions, Exhibiting "The Truth" in Opposition to the Dogmas of Papal and Protestant Christendom* (Birmingham: Frank G. Jannaway, 1920; repr., Houston, TX: Herald, n.d.) iv, http://www.antipas.org/pdf_files/christadelphian_answers.pdf.
10. Jannaway, *Christadelphian Answers*, 182.
11. Jannaway, *Christadelphian Answers*, 183.
12. Jannaway, *Christadelphian Answers*, 193.

13. Jannaway, *Christadelphian Answers*, v.
14. Jannaway, *Christadelphian Answers*, 297.
15. Jannaway, *Christadelphian Answers*, 190–191.
16. Jannaway, *Christadelphian Answers*, 192.
17. Lippy, *The Christadelphians in North America*, 82–83.
18. Harry Tennant, *The Christadelphians: What They Believe and Preach*, 2nd ed. (Birmingham: The Christadelphian, 1988), vii.
19. Lippy, *The Christadelphians in North America*, 126.
20. Harry Whittaker, "Block Disfellowship: Is It Taught in the Bible? (1)," *The Testimony Magazine*, August 1973, 310.
21. Whittaker, "Block Disfellowship (1)," 310.
22. Whittaker, "Block Disfellowship (1)," 313.
23. Harry Whittaker, "Block Disfellowship (2)," *The Testimony Magazine*, September 1973, 343.
24. Whittaker, "Block Disfellowship (2)," 344–345. The "Constitution" Whittaker speaks of here is none other than Robert Roberts's "Ecclesial Guide."
25. Jannaway, *Christadelphian Answers*, iv-v; and Whittaker, "Block Disfellow-ship (2)," 344–345.
26. For more on this controversy, see Lippy, *The Christadelphians in North America*, 68–73.
27. J.J. Andrew, "Sin and Its Removal, as Taught by Dr. Thomas," *The Sanctu-ary-Keeper*, March 1895, 111.
28. Andrew, "Sin and Its Removal, as Taught by Dr. Thomas," 112.
29. Islip Collyer, *Letters to Young Christadelphians* (Adelaide, South Australia: Committee of the 21st Australasian Christadelphian Youth Conference, 1991), 15.
30. Alan Eyre, *The Protesters* (Birmingham: The Christadelphian, 1975), 8. Eyre's attempt to locate Christadelphians scattered throughout the distant past resembles similar efforts undertaken by the Landmark Baptists. For more on that group, see James A. Patterson, "Reframing the Past: The Impact of Institutional and Ideological Agendas on Modern Interpretations of Landmarkism," in *Through a Glass Darkly: Contested Notions of Baptist Identity*, ed. Keith Harper (Tuscaloosa, AL: University of Alabama Press, 2012), 228–250.
31. Eyre, *The Protesters*, 9.
32. Ruth McHaffie, *Brethren Indeed?: Christadelphians and "Outsiders" (16th-21st century)* (Ian McHaffie, 2001), 3–4, http://www.christadelphianbooks.org/books.html.
33. McHaffie, *Brethren Indeed?*, 5.
34. Thomas Gaston, "Proto-Christadelphians," *Christadelphian eJournal of Biblical Interpretation* 3, no. 2 (April 2009): 37.

35. Al Diestelkamp, "The Unfinished Work of Restoration," *Think on these Things*, April-May-June 2001, 1.
36. Tant is referring to Nehemiah 13:23–24, which criticizes the postexilic Israelite men who married women from surrounding tribes, including Ashdod, and failed to teach their children to speak their native tongue of Hebrew.
37. Fanning Yater Tant, "Denominationalism?" in *What is Wrong? Containing ten speeches of Vickery Boulevard, Fort Worth, Texas Lectureship of October 30 to November 6, 1949 and four special contributions*, ed. Thomas L. Campbell (Fort Worth, TX: Campbell-Caskey Publishing Co., 1950), 128.
38. Melvin Curry, Walking in the Old Paths," in *Reemphasizing Bible Basics in Current Controversies: Florida College Annual Lectures, 1990*, ed. Melvin D. Curry (Temple Terrace, FL: Florida College Bookstore, 1990), 7–8.
39. Hoyt Houchen, "The Work of the Church," in *Reemphasizing Bible Basics in Current Controversies: Florida College Annual Lectures, 1990*, ed. Melvin D. Curry (Temple Terrace, FL: Florida College Bookstore, 1990), 134–135.
40. Fanning Yater Tant, *J.D. Tant—Texas Preacher: A Biography* (Erlanger, KY: Faith and Facts Press, 1958), 7–8.
41. Homer Hailey, "Shall History Repeat Itself?" *Bible Banner*, May 1941, 6, http://www.wordsfitlyspoken.org/bible_banner/v3/v3n10p6.html.
42. Harry R. Osborne, "Set for the Defense of the Gospel: Protecting the Local Church," *Watchman Magazine*, November 1997, http://watchmanmag.com/0000/000013.htm.
43. Houchen, "The Work of the Church," 121.
44. Tom Roberts, "Associate Editorial: Attitudes Toward the Preaching of the Gospel," *Watchman Magazine*, November 1997, http://watchmanmag.-com/0000/000001.htm.
45. Marty Wooten, "Editorial," *Biblical Discipleship Quarterly: The International Magazine for Growing Christians*, Spring Quarter 1987, 3.
46. Bob Gempel, "Remnant Theology," *Boston Bulletin*, October 25, 1987, 1, 7.
47. Gordon Ferguson, *Prepared to Answer* (Woburn, MA: Discipleship Publications International, 1995), 121.
48. Hughes, *Reviving the Ancient Faith*, 358–359.
49. Stanback, *Into All Nations*, 36.
50. Jerry Jones, *Back to the Basics* (Bridgeton, MO: Mid-America Book and Tape Sales, 1988), 5.
51. Thomas A. Jones, *In Search of a City: An Autobiographical Perspective on a Remarkable but Controversial Movement* (Spring Hill, TN: DPI Books, 2007), 11, 18.
52. David Harrington Watt, *Bible-Carrying Christians: Conservative Protestants and Social Power* (New York: Oxford University Press, 2002), 86–87.

53. The version of "Revolution Through Restoration" that I am using contains all three articles in one PDF file. The page numbers I cite here and elsewhere refer to the page count of the specific article referenced, not the page count of the document as a whole. Kip McKean, "Revolution Through Restoration I: From Jerusalem to Rome, From Boston to Moscow," 15. http://www.usd21.org/wp-content/uploads/2012/06/Revolution_Through_Restoration.pdf.
54. McKean, "From Jerusalem to Rome, From Boston to Moscow," 25, 20. McKean argues that in the same way that the church at Thessalonica was commended as a model for those at Macedonia and Achaia, so too could the church at Los Angeles serve as a model for others within the ICOC.
55. McKean, "From Jerusalem to Rome, From Boston to Moscow," 15.
56. Alvin Jennings, ed., *Introducing the Church of Christ: Distinctive Features of the Church of Christ Discussed By Over Fifty of Her Ministers* (Fort Worth, TX: Star Bible Publications, Inc., 1981).
57. Alvin Jennings, *How Christianity Grows in the City* (Fort Worth, TX: Star Bible Publications, 1985), 2, 138.
58. The reasons for McKean's removal are the subject of some debate, but Stanback (*Into All Nations*, 121) argues that "the catalyst for the decision stemmed primarily from the spiritual struggles of one of his children, now a sophomore at Harvard, who was questioning her beliefs and had recently stopped attending church services."
59. Jenkins, *Awesome Families*, 246; Stanback, *Into All Nations*, 141–142.
60. Ron Harding, *The Chronicles of Modern-Day Christianity* (Columbia, SC: SoldOut Press International, 2018), 103.
61. Harding, *Chronicles of Modern-Day Christianity*, 13.
62. Harding, *Chronicles of Modern-Day Christianity*, 13.
63. Harding, *Chronicles of Modern-Day Christianity*, 32–33.
64. Harding, *Chronicles of Modern-Day Christianity*, 98.
65. Harding, *Chronicles of Modern-Day Christianity*, 83.
66. Harding, *Chronicles of Modern-Day Christianity*, 14.
67. **Mark Driscoll, "A Pastoral Perspective on the Emergent Church," *Criswell Theological Review* 3, no. 2 (Spring 2006): 92.**
68. Kester Brewin, *Signs of Emergence: A Vision for Church That is Organic/Networked/Decentralized/Bottom-Up/Communal/Flexible/Always Evolving* (Grand Rapids, MI: Baker Books, 2007), 12.
69. Ray S. Anderson, *An Emergent Theology for Emerging Churches* (Downers Grove, IL: IVP Books, 2006), 85–86.

EPILOGUE

1. As a little nod to the influence of Douglas Hofstadter on my thinking about recursion, I very loosely modeled Chapter Four on his discussion of the "Little Harmonic Labyrinth," a piece of music so known because its rapid succession of key changes leaves most listeners unable to determine whether or not it has properly "resolved" by the end—a fitting way to structure a chapter on a process that seems to still be taking place, I think. For that discussion, as well as one of my favorite short stories/dialogues, see Hofstadter, *Gödel, Escher, Bach*, 103–152.
2. DeGroot, *The Restoration Principle*, 20, 8.
3. RoseAnn Benson, *Alexander Campbell and Joseph Smith: 19th-Century Restorationists* (Provo, UT: Brigham Young University Press, 2017); John G. Turner, *The Mormon Jesus: A Biography* (Cambridge, MA: Belknap Press, 2016).
4. Admittedly, "ecclesiology" may not be quite the right word for political history, but the underlying concept remains valid nonetheless.
5. Fea, *Believe Me*, 165–178. Fehrman notes that "A love of American history is as old as America itself, and each generation has tried to define its values, and to sell its policies, by citing that history." Additionally, he contends, "Americans like to collapse the past and the present, to read for serious ideas and for hero worship." See Craig Fehrman, *Author in Chief: The Untold Story of Our Presidents and the Books They Wrote* (New York: Avid Reader Press, 2020), 4.
6. Randall J. Stephens, *The Fire Spreads: Holiness and Pentecostalism in the American South* (Cambridge, MA: Harvard University Press, 2008), 149.
7. Stephens, *The Fire Spreads*, 214.
8. One scholar has written that "Pentecostalism's recent history is littered with 'revival' movements causing multiple schisms that have almost become its defining feature." See A.H. Anderson, "Pentecostalism," in *Evangelical Dictionary of Theology*, 3rd ed., ed. Daniel J. Treier and Walter A. Elwell (Grand Rapids, MI: Baker Academic, 2017), 649.
9. DeGroot, *The Restoration Principle*, 125.
10. Julia Stewart Werner, *The Primitive Methodist Connexion: Its Background and Early History* (Madison, WI: The University of Wisconsin Press, 1984), 15. See also Tim Woolley, "A Community of Selective Memory? Hugh Bourne, William Clowes and Primitive Methodist Historiography," *Wesley and Methodist Studies* 2 (2010): 67–90.
11. Roy B. Ward, "'The Restoration Principle': A Critical Analysis," *Restoration Quarterly* 8, no. 4 (1965): 197.

BIBLIOGRAPHY

Articles

Adams, Donna L. "Brief Report: Perceived Psychological Abuse and the Cincinnati Church of Christ." *Cultic Studies Journal* 15, no. 1 (1998): 87–88.

Ahlstrom, Sydney E. "The Scottish Philosophy and American Theology." *Church History* 24, no. 3 (September 1955): 257–272.

Alexander, Peter. "'I will give you the man': Paton's Spirituality." *Scrutiny 2: Issues in English Studies in South Africa* 16, no. 1 (2011), 7–18.

Alnor, William M. and Ronald Enroth. "Ethical Problems in Exit Counseling." *Christian Research Journal* (Winter 1992): 14–19.

Altholz, Josef L. "Anonymity and Editorial Responsibility in Religious Journalism." *Victorian Periodicals Review* 24, no. 4 (Winter 1991): 180–186.

Avis, Paul. "Editorial." *Ecclesiology* 1, no. 1 (September 2004): 6–7.

Baird, A.W. III. "Determination of Electron Density Profiles from Tonks-Dattner Resonance Data in Plasmas." *Journal of Applied Physics* 42, no. 13 (December 1971): 5358–5361.

Baird, A.W. III and D.G. Swanson. "Experimental Investigation of the Ion-Ion Hybrid Resonance." *The Physics of Fluids* 12, no. 9 (September 1969): 1878–1885.

Baker, William R. "Addendum to 'Coming Full Circle: Biblical Scholarship in Christian Churches.'" *Stone-Campbell Journal* 11, no. 1 (Spring 2008): 93–95.

Baker, William R., Paul J. Kissling, and Tony Springer. "Coming Full Circle: Biblical Scholarship in Christian Churches." *Stone-Campbell Journal* 10, no. 2 (Fall 2007): 165–191.

Baumel, Judith Tydor. "Twice a Refugee: The Jewish Refugee Children in Great Britain during Evacuation, 1939-1943." *Jewish Social Studies* 45, no. 2 (Spring 1983): 175–184.

Bergman, Jerry. "The Modern Religious Objection to Mandatory Flag Salute in America: A History and Evaluation." *Journal of Church and State* 39, no. 2 (Spring 1997): 215–236.

Bolt, John. "An Emerging Critique of the Postmodern, Evangelical Church: A Review Essay." *Calvin Theological Journal* 41, no. 2 (November 2006): 205–221.

Branch, Rick. "Boston Church of Christ/International Church of Christ." *Watchman Fellowship Profile*, 1993. https://www.watchman.org/profiles/pdf/icocprofile.pdf

Burge, Ryan P., and Paul A. Djupe. "Truly Inclusive or Uniformly Liberal? An Analysis of the Politics of the Emerging Church." *Journal for the Scientific Study of Religion* 53, no. 3 (September 2014): 636–651.

Cantrell, Gregg. "Lyndon's Granddaddy: Samuel Ealy

Johnson Sr., Texas Populism, and the Improbable Roots of American Liberalism." *Southwestern Historical Quarterly* 118 (2014): 132–156.

Carrillo, Robert. "The International Churches of Christ (ICOC)." *Leaven* 17, no. 3 (Third Quarter 2009): 151–156.

Chinn, Stuart. "Institutional Recalibration and Judicial Delimitation." *Law & Social Inquiry* 37, no. 3 (Summer 2012): 535–564.

Clark, Ron. "Pendleton, Franklin, Sommer, and Ketcherside: Mutual Edification in our Roots to Build Up the Body." *Restoration Quarterly* 51, no. 3 (2009): 151–168.

Clementson, Julian. "The Christadelphians and the Doctrine of the Trinity." *Evangelical Quarterly* 75, no. 2 (April 2003): 157–176.

Coady, C.A.J. "The Socinian Connection: Further Thoughts on the Religion of Hobbes." *Religious Studies* 22, no. 2 (June 1986): 277–280.

Coates, Dominiek D. "A symbolic interactionist understanding of the selves of former members of New Religious Movements." *Mental Health, Religion & Culture* 16, no. 10 (December 2013): 1066–1079.

———. "Life Inside a Deviant 'Religious' Group: Conformity and Commitment Asensured through 'Brainwashing' or as the Result of Normal Processes of Socialisation." *International Journal of Law, Crime and Justice* 44 (March 2016): 103–121.

——— "New Religious Movement Membership and the Importance of Stable 'Others' for the Making of Selves." *Journal of Religious Health* 53, no. 5 (April 2013): 1300–1316.

Cotten, Chris. "'The Center and Stronghold of Our Cause in Alabama': Early Stone-Campbell History in Birmingham, Alabama, 1874-1908." *Restoration Quarterly* 59, no. 3 (2017): 141–155.

Coulson, Derek. "The Cost of Compromise: The Legacy of J.W. McGarvey." *Restoration Quarterly* 61, no. 1 (2019): 13–26.

Driscoll, Mark. "A Pastoral Perspective on the Emergent Church." *Criswell Theological Review* 3, no. 2 (Spring 2006): 87–93.

Eliot, T.S. "Milton." *The Sewanee Review* 56, no. 2 (Spring 1948): 185–209.

Ellett, Kent. "Non-Sunday School Churches of Christ: Their Origins and Transformation." *Discipliana* 60, no. 2 (Summer 2000): 49–63.

Eremicheva, G.V. "Religious Searching and New Religious Organizations (On the Example of the Church of Christ in St. Petersburg)." *Anthropology & Archeology of Eurasia* 47, no. 4 (Spring 2009): 9–34.

Fikes, Jason. "Emerging Historiography: How Church Leaders Are Looking at the Past and Shaping What Is to Come." *Stone-Campbell Journal* 14, no. 2 (Fall 2011): 207–218.

Foster, Douglas. "Stephen D. Eckstein Jr. and Churches of Christ: 1950-2001." *Restoration Quarterly* 43, no. 4 (2001): 199–210.

Froese, Vic. "The Emerging Church: A Select Bibliography." *Direction* 39, no. 1 (Spring 2010): 106–112.

Gaustad, Edwin S. "EDITORIAL: Barbarians and Memory." *Journal of Church and State* 37, no. 1 (Winter 1995): 7–13.

Geach, Peter. "The Religion of Thomas Hobbes." *Religious Studies* 17, no. 4 (December 1981): 549–558.

Graziani, Carlo, Robert Rosner, Jennifer M. Adams, and Reason L. Machete. "Probabilistic Recalibration of Forecasts." Working paper, 2019. http://arxiv.org/abs/1904.02855.

Guest, Mathew. “The Emerging Church in Transatlantic Perspective.” *Journal for the Scientific Study of Religion* 56, no. 1 (March 2017): 41–51.

Hall, N.A. “W. and J. Birkenhead ‘Ferns a Specialty.’” *Garden History* 11, no. 1 (Spring 1983): 79–85.

Hamilton, Mark W. “Transition and Continuity: Biblical Scholarship in Today’s Churches of Christ.” *Stone-Campbell Journal* 9, no. 2 (Fall 2006): 187–203.

Hammett, John S. “An Ecclesiological Assessment of the Emerging Church.” *Criswell Theological Review* 3, no. 2 (Spring 2006): 29–49.

Handasyde, Kerrie. “Pioneering Leadership: Historical Myth-Making, Absence, and Identity in the Churches of Christ in Victoria.” *Journal of Religious History* 41, no. 2 (June 2017): 235–250.

———“Transforming History: The Origins of the Stone-Campbell Movement in Victoria, Australia.” *Stone-Campbell Journal* 17, no. 1 (Spring 2014): 3–18.

Hart, Larry. “Brief History of a Minor Restorationist Group (The Non-Sunday-School Churches of Christ).” *Restoration Quarterly* 22, no. 4 (1979): 212–232.

Hill, Samuel S. “David Edwin Harrell Jr.: American Religious Historian.” *Restoration Quarterly* 46, no. 3 (2004): 225–234.

Hughes, Richard T. “Twenty-Five Years of Restoration Scholarship: The Churches of Christ, Part I.” *Restoration Quarterly* 25, no. 4 (1982): 233–256.

——— “Twenty-Five Years of Restoration Scholarship: The Churches of Christ, Part II.” *Restoration Quarterly* 26, no. 1 (1983): 39–62.

Ioannidis, John P.A. “Why Most Published Research

Findings Are False." *PLoS Medicine* 2, no.8 (August 2005): 696–701.

Jackman, Graham. "'Ich Kann Nicht Zwei Herren Dienen': Conscientious Objectors and Nazi 'Militärjustiz': The Undocumented Cases of Three Brothers." *German Life and Letters* 64, no. 2 (April 2011): 188–216.

Jenkins, Kathleen E. "Intimate Diversity: The Presentation of Multiculturalism and Multiracialism in a High-Boundary Religious Movement." *Journal for the Scientific Study of Religion* 42, no. 3 (September 2003): 393–409.

Jeter, Joseph R. Jr. "Some We Lost: A Study of Disaffections from the Disciples of Christ." *Discipliana* 61, no. 1 (Spring 2001): 3–30.

Láng, Benedek. "Ciphers in Magic: Techniques of Revelation and Concealment." *Magic, Ritual, and Witchcraft* 10, no. 2 (Winter 2015): 125–141.

Langford, Thomas A. "An Insider's View of non-Sunday school Churches of Christ." *Restoration Quarterly* 45, no. 3 (2003): 181–192.

Lightfoot, Marguerita, Mary Jane Rotheram-Borus, Belinda Towns, Timothy R. Cline, Douglas Webber, Debra A. Murphy, and Lan Feng Tsai. "Religious Groups as Diffusers of HIV Antibody Testing and Prevention Messages." *Journal of Community Psychology* 29, no. 4 (July 2001): 459–472.

Little, David L. "Inductive Hermeneutics and the Early Restoration Movement." *Stone-Campbell Journal* 3, no.1 (Spring 2000): 5–18.

Looney, Jared. "Metropolis: A Stone-Campbell Mosaic." *Leaven* 17, no. 3 (Third Quarter 2009): 136–140.

Love, D'Esta and Stuart Love, eds. "International

Churches of Christ." Special issue, *Leaven: A Publication of Ministry for Churches of the Restoration Heritage* 18, no. 2 (Second Quarter 2010).

Malloy, Patrick. "Rick Warren Meets Gregory Dix: The Liturgical Movement Comes Knocking at the Megachurch Door." *Anglican Theological Review* 92, no. 3 (Summer 2010): 439–453.

Matson, David Lertis. "'I Have Brothers and Sisters in Those Parties': More on the 'Conscientious Sister' of the Lunenburg Letter." *Stone-Campbell Journal* 14, no. 2 (Fall 2011): 165–188.

——— "Who Wrote the Lunenburg Letter? The Untold Story of the 'Conscientious Sister' of Lunenburg." *Stone-Campbell Journal* 11, no. 1 (Spring 2008): 3–28.

Mayhue, Richard L. "The Emerging Church: Generous Orthodoxy or General Obfuscation?" *The Master's Seminary Journal* 17, no. 2 (Fall 2006): 191–205.

McKinzie, Greg, ed. "Missional. Monastic. Restorationist?" Special issue, *Missio Dei: A Journal of Missional Theology and Praxis* 9, no. 2 (Summer—Fall 2018). http://missiodeijournal.com/?fbclid=IwAR0BLUP28grrtLyiEVAuPxcU-Uzuhp4utT5pBlzCUzs5E9592d_TfXmdjo4E

Michael, Kelsey Sherrod. "Wearing Your Heart on Your Sleeve: The Surveillance of Women's Souls in Evangelical Christian Modesty Culture." *Feminist Media Studies* 19, no. 8 (2019): 1129–1143.

Moritz, Joshua M. "Beyond Strategy, Towards the Kingdom of God." *Dialog: A Journal of Theology* 47, no. 1 (Spring 2008): 27–36.

Năstuţă, Sebastian. "The Impact of Internet on New Religious Movements' Discourse." *Sociologie Românească* 10, no. 4 (2012): 61–74.

Nugent, John C. "Was Alexander Campbell Enslaved to Scottish Baconianism?" *Stone-Campbell Journal* 12, no. 1 (Spring 2009): 15–30.

Oden, Patrick. "An Emerging Pneumatology: Jürgen Moltmann and the Emerging Church in Conversation." *Journal of Pentecostal Theology* 18, no. 2 (September 2009): 263–284.

Packard, Josh. "Resisting Institutionalization: Religious Professionals in the Emerging Church." *Sociological Inquiry* 81, no. 1 (February 2011): 3–33.

Paden, Glenn. "The Lunenburg Letter: An Incident in the History of the Interpretation of Baptism." *Restoration Quarterly* 2, no. 1 (1958): 13–18.

Perry, Lowell. "History of Broadcasting in Churches of Christ From 1922-1953." *Restoration Quarterly* 18, no. 1 (1975): 34–40.

Perry, Seth. "Scripture, Time, and Authority among Early Disciples of Christ." *Church History* 85, no. 4 (December 2016): 762–783.

Pettegrew, Larry D. "Evangelicalism, Paradigms, and the Emerging Church." *The Master's Seminary Journal* 17, no. 2 (Fall 2006) 159–175.

Piper, Sophie K., Ulrike Grittner, Andre Rex, Nico Riedel, Felix Fischer, Robert Nadon, Bob Siegerink, and Ulrich Dirnagl. "Exact Replication: Foundation of Science or Game of Chance?" *PLoS Biology* 17, no. 4 (2019).

Rambo, Lewis R. "Congregational Care and Discipline in the San Francisco Church of Christ: A Case Study." *Pastoral Psychology* 43, no. 4 (March 1995): 283–298.

Riddle, Paul W. "An Annotated Bibliography of Articles on Restoration History Published in *Restoration Quarterly* from 1957 to 1983." *Restoration Quarterly* 28, no. 4 (1985–1986): 235–247.

Roberts, Wesley. "The Hymnody of Christadelphians: A Survey of Hymnists and Hymn Collections." *The Hymn: A Journal of Congregational Song* 48, no. 3 (July 1997): 44–51.

Ross, Margaret Ann. "Early Camp Meetings in Faulkner County, Arkansas." *The Arkansas Historical Quarterly* 10, no. 2 (Summer 1951): 157–167.

Sensing, Timothy R. "Baconian Method and Preaching in the Stone-Campbell Movement." *Stone-Campbell Journal* 4, no. 2 (Fall 2001): 163–185.

Shrock, Christopher A. "Culpability and Conscience: A Philosophical Look at an Early Restoration Theme." *Restoration Quarterly* 61, no. 3 (2019): 143–156.

Shults, F. Leron. "Reforming Ecclesiology in Emerging Churches." *Theology Today* 65, no. 4 (January 2009): 425–438.

Smith, R. Scott. "Some Suggestions for Brian McLaren (and His Critics)." *Criswell Theological Review* 3, no. 2 (Spring 2006): 67–85.

Stanczak, Gregory C. "Strategic Ethnicity: The Construction of Multi-racial/Multi-ethnic Religious Community." *Ethnic and Racial Studies* 29, no. 5 (September 2006): 856–881.

Wah, Carolyn R. "Restrictions on Religious Training and Exposure in Child Custody and Visitation Orders: Do They Protect or Harm the Child?" *Journal of Church and State* 45, no. 4 (Autumn 2003): 765–785.

Ward, Roy B. "'The Restoration Principle': A Critical Analysis." *Restoration Quarterly* 8, no. 4 (1965): 197–210.

Walker, Philip A., Jr. "Lyndon B. Johnson's Senate Foreign

Policy Activism: The Suez Canal Crisis, a Reappraisal." *Presidential Studies Quarterly* 26, no. 4 (Fall 1996): 996–1008.

Warren, David H. "The Men of Glasgow: Influences Upon the Campbells." *Restoration Quarterly* 51, no. 2 (2009): 65–79.

Wilson, Bryan R. "Ever on the watch." Review of *The Christadelphians in North America*, by Charles H. Lippy. *Times Literary Supplement*, May 18, 1990, 531.

Wollschleger, Jason. "Disengaged *and* Indistinct: The Subcultural Identity of the Emerging Church Movement." *Social Compass* 62, no. 1 (March 2015): 105–121.

Woolley, Tim. "A Community of Selective Memory? Hugh Bourne, William Clowes and Primitive Methodist Historiography." *Wesley and Methodist Studies* 2 (2010): 67–90.

Yi, Joseph. "The Dynamics of Liberal Indifference and Inclusion in a Global Era." *Society* 52 (June 2015): 264–274.

Young, John. "Christadelphian Blueprints for Restoring the Early Church, 1848-1920." *Stone Campbell Journal* 22, no. 2 (Fall 2019): 165–177.

Yust, Karen-Marie. "The Construction of Denominational Identity by Negation: The Separation of the Stone-Campbell Movements from the Baptists and Presbyterians." *Discipliana* 63, no. 3 (Fall 2003): 93–96.

Books

Abel, Ron. *Wrested Scriptures: A Christadelphian Handbook of Suggested Explanations to Difficult Passages*. Pasadena, CA: Geddes Press, n.d. http://www.christadelphian.or.tz/sites/default/files/wrested_scriptures.pdf.

Adams, Lindy and Scott LaMascus, eds. *Decades of*

Destiny: A History of Churches of Christ from 1900-2000. Abilene, TX: ACU Press, 2004.

Ahlstrom, Sydney E. *A Religious History of the American People*. New Haven, CT: Yale University Press, 1972.

Allen, C. Leonard and Richard T. Hughes. *Discovering Our Roots: The Ancestry of Churches of Christ*. Abilene, TX: ACU Press, 1988.

Allen, C. Leonard, Richard T. Hughes, and Michael R. Weed. *The Worldly Church: A Call for Biblical Renewal*. Abilene, TX: ACU Press, 1988.

Allen, C. Leonard and Danny Gray Swick. *Participating in God's Life: Two Crossroads for Churches of Christ*. Orange, CA: New Leaf Books, 2001.

Alward, Peter. *Empty Revelations: An Essay on Talk about, and Attitudes toward, Fiction*. Montreal: McGill-Queen's University Press, 2012.

Anderson, James. *An Outline of My Life, or Selections from a Fifty Years' Religious Experience*,1912. http://www.simply-christians.co.uk/eusebos/eusebos/zpayne1/andersl1.htm.

Anderson, Ray S. *An Emergent Theology for Emerging Churches*. Downers Grove, IL: IVP Books, 2006.

Andrew, J.J. *The Blood of the Covenant*. Fifth ed. Richmond, VA: Christadelphian Publications, 1985. http://www.christadelphianaudio.org/books/ Andrew_BloodoftheCovenant.pdf.

———. *The Doctrine of the Atonement: An Expository Lecture Delivered in May, 1882, in Wellington Hall, Islington, London*. 1987 ed. Richmond, VA: Christadelphian Publications, 1987. http://literature.christadelphianresources.-com/Andrew/ Doctrine%20of%20the%20Atonent.PDF.

———. *The Real Christ*. 1948 ed. Loughborough, UK:

Echo Press Ltd., 1948. http://christadelphianbooks.org/books.html.

Baker, William R., ed. *Evangelicalism and the Stone-Campbell Movement*. Downers Grove, IL: InterVarsity Press, 2002.

Banta, Joseph. *The Apocalypse: A Background Study*. Dearborn, MI: PAK Printers, Inc., 1985. http://christadelphianbooks.org/ books.html.

Barnett, Maurice. *The Discipling Movement: A Study of the Neo-Crossroads Philosophy among Churches of Christ*. 2nd ed. Phoenix, AZ: Maurice Barnett, 1989.

Bauer, Rick. *Toxic Christianity: The International Church of Christ/Boston Movement*. Bowie, MD: Freedom House Ministries, 1994.

Bauer, Sarah. *A Time to Speak: A Personal Journal of My Years in the Boston Movement*. 2nd ed. Upper Marlboro, MD: Freedom House, 1993.

Beale, Maurice. *Notes on Systematic Prophecy*. Wanganui, New Zealand: Maurice Beale, 2004. http://menuchabibleschool.org/ 2000/MaurieBeale/mb2000Handout.pdf.

Bell, Rob. *Drops Like Stars*. Grand Rapids, MI: Zondervan, 2009.

———. *Love Wins: A Book About Heaven, Hell, and the Fate of Every Person Who Ever Lived*. New York: HarperOne, 2011.

———. *The Love Wins Companion: A Study Guide for Those Who Want to Go Deeper*. Edited by David Vanderveen. New York: HarperOne, 2011.

———. *Millones Cajones: A Novel*. Published by author, 2015. PDF e-book.

———. *Sex God: Exploring the Endless Connections Between Sexuality and Spirituality*. Grand Rapids, MI: Zondervan, 2007.

———. *Velvet Elvis: Repainting the Christian Faith*. Grand Rapids, MI: Zondervan, 2005.

———. *What Is the Bible? How an Ancient Library of Poems, Letters, and Stories Can Transform the Way You Think and Feel About Everything*. New York: HarperOne, 2017.

———. *What We Talk About When We Talk About God*. New York: HarperOne, 2013.

Bell, Rob, and Don Golden. *Jesus Wants to Save Christians: A Manifesto for the Church in Exile*. Grand Rapids, MI: Zondervan, 2008.

Ben-Yehuda, Nachman and Amalya Oliver-Lumerman. *Fraud and Misconduct in Research: Detection, Investigation, and Organizational Response*. Ann Arbor, MI: University of Michigan Press, 2017.

Benson, RoseAnn. *Alexander Campbell and Joseph Smith: 19th-Century Restorationists*. Provo, UT: Brigham Young University Press, 2017.

Bielo, James S. *Emerging Evangelicals: Faith, Modernity, and the Desire for Authenticity*. NewYork: New York University Press, 2011.

Bloom, Harold. *The American Religion: The Emergence of the Post-Christian Nation*. NewYork: Simon & Schuster, 1992.

Bolger, Ryan K., ed. *The Gospel after Christendom: New Voices, New Cultures, New Expressions*. Grand Rapids, MI: Baker Academic, 2012.

Bolz-Weber, Nadia. *Accidental Saints: Finding God in All the Wrong People*. New York: Convergent Books, 2015.

———. *Pastrix: The Cranky, Beautiful Faith of a Sinner & Saint*. New York: Jericho Books, 2013.

———. *Salvation on the Small Screen?: 24 Hours of Christian Television*. NewYork: Seabury Books, 2008.

Bowers, Calvin H. *Realizing the California Dream: The Story of Black Churches of Christ in Los Angeles*. Calvin H. Bowers, 2001.

Brewin, Kester. *Signs of Emergence: A Vision for Church That is Organic/Networked/Decentralized/Bottom-Up/Communal/Flexible/Always Evolving*. Grand Rapids, MI: Baker Books, 2007.

Brice, Tanya Smith, ed. *Reconciliation Reconsidered: Advancing the National Conversation on Race in Churches of Christ*. Abilene, TX: Abilene Christian University Press, 2016.

Brownlow, Leroy. *Why I am a Member of the Church of Christ*. Fort Worth, TX: The Brownlow Corporation, 2012.

Burson, Scott R. *Brian McLaren in Focus: A New Kind of Apologetics*. Abilene, TX: Abilene Christian University Press, 2016.

Camp, Lee C. *Mere Discipleship: Radical Christianity in a Rebellious World*. 2nd ed. Grand Rapids, MI: Brazos Press, 2008.

Campbell, Heidi A., ed. *Digital Religion: Understanding Religious Practice in New Media Worlds*. New York: Routledge, 2013.

Campbell, Thomas L., ed. *What is Wrong? Containing Ten Speeches of Vickery Boulevard, Fort Worth, Texas Lectureship of October 30 to November 6, 1949 and Four Special Contributions*. Fort Worth, TX: Campbell-Caskey Publishing Co., 1950.

Carey, Patrick W. and Joseph T. Lienhard, eds. *Biographical Dictionary of Christian Theologians*. Peabody, MA: Hendrickson Publishers, Inc., 2002.

Carson, D.A. *Becoming Conversant with the Emerging Church: Understanding a Movement and Its Implications*. Grand Rapids, MI: Zondervan, 2005.

———. *Exegetical Fallacies*. 2nd ed. Grand Rapids, MI: Baker Academic, 1996. Logos Bible Software.

Casey, Michael W. *Saddlebags, City Streets, and Cyberspace: A History of Preaching in the Churches of Christ*. Abilene, TX: ACU Press, 1995.

Casey, Michael W. and Douglas A. Foster, eds. *The Stone-Campbell Movement: An International Religious Tradition*. Knoxville, TN: The University of Tennessee Press, 2002.

Chan, Francis and Preston Sprinkle: *Erasing Hell: What God Said About Eternity, and the Things We've Made Up*. Colorado Springs, CO: David C Cook, 2011.

Childers, Jeff W., Douglas A. Foster, and Jack R. Reese. *The Crux of the Matter: Crisis, Tradition, and the Future of Churches of Christ*. Abilene, TX: ACU Press, 2001.

Claiborne, Shane. *The Irresistible Revolution: Living as an Ordinary Radical*. Grand Rapids, MI: Zondervan, 2006.

Clanton, J. Caleb. *The Philosophy of Religion of Alexander Campbell*. Knoxville, TN: The University of Tennessee Press, 2013.

Clawson, Michael, and April Stace, eds. *Crossing Boundaries, Redefining Faith: Interdisciplinary Perspectives on the Emerging Church Movement*. Eugene, OR: Wipf & Stock Publishers, 2016.

Cogdill, Roy E. *The Origins and Claims of Roman Catholicism*. Fayette, AL: The Marion Davis Company, n.d.

Coleman, Robert E. *The Master Plan of Evangelism*. 2nd ed., abr. Grand Rapids, MI: Revell, 2010.

Coleman, Robert and Bobby Harrington. *Revisiting the Master Plan of Evangelism: Why Jesus' Discipleship Method is Still the Best Today*. With Josh Patrick. Renew, 2014. PDF.

Collyer, Islip. *Conviction and Conduct: The Faith that*

Works. Birmingham: The Christadelphian, 1968. http://christadelphianbooks.org/books.html.

———. *Letters to Young Christadelphians*. Adelaide, South Australia: Committee of the 21st Australasian Christadelphian Youth Conference, 1991. http://christadelphianbooks.org/ books.html.

———. *"Vox Dei": A Defence of Simple Faith: Presenting the Real Case for the Bible and Explaining the Obstinacy of the Stalwarts who know all that can be urged against the Bible far better than some of the Critics, but who Remain Absolutely Convinced that it is The Word of God*. Birmingham: C.C. Walker, 1921. http://christadelphianbooks.org/books.html.

Conkin, Paul K. *American Originals: Homemade Varieties of Christianity*. Chapel Hill, NC: The University of North Carolina Press, 1997.

Cook, Jim. *The Myth of the Stone-Campbell Movement*. Lanham, MD: Lexington Books, 2019.

Cowie, J.A. *Conscientious Objection to Military Service: A Manual Designed to Assist Christadelphian Young People Facing the Prospect of a National Service Call-Up*. Hawthorndene, South Australia: Christadelphian Scripture Study Service, 1999. http://christadelphianbooks.org/books.html.

Cox, John D. *A Concise Account of Church History with Questions for Group Study*. Murfreesboro, TN: Dehoff Publications, 1997.

———. *A Word Fitly Spoken: Autobiography, Sermons, Lectures, Articles, Scrapbook Gleanings*. Nashville, TN: Gospel Advocate Company, 1962.

Crawford, Aleck. *The Spirit: A General Exposition on New Testament Usage*. Internet ed. Hallett Cove, South Australia.

The WORD Typeset, 2001. http://www.thechristadelphians.org/ btcd/downloads/pdf/The_Spirit_Internet_Edition.pdf.

Crawford, Wes. *Shattering the Illusion: How African American Churches of Christ Moved from Segregation to Independence.* Abilene, TX: Abilene Christian University Press, 2013.

Curry, Melvin D., ed. *Reemphasizing Bible Basics in Current Controversies: Florida College Annual Lectures, 1990.* Temple Terrace, FL: Florida College Bookstore, 1990.

———, ed. *They Being Dead Yet Speak: Florida College Annual Lectures, 1981.* Temple Terrace, FL: Florida College Bookstore, 1981.

Dabney-Frost Debate on Marriage, Divorce, and Remarriage: Must Adulterers Separate Before Being Baptized? Fort Worth, TX: The Manney Company, 1959.

Deffenbaugh, Donald R. *The Discipling Movement Among Churches of Christ.* Neosho, MO: Donald R. Deffenbaugh, 1986.

DeGroot, Alfred T. *Church of Christ Number Two.* Birmingham, England: The Birmingham Printers, 1956.

———. *The Restoration Principle.* St. Louis, MO: The Bethany Press, 1960.

DeYoung, Kevin, and Ted Kluck. *Why We're Not Emergent (By Two Guys Who Should Be).* Chicago: Moody Publishers, 2008.

Dochuk, Darren. *From Bible Belt to Sunbelt: Plain-Folk Religion, Grassroots Politics, and the Rise of Evangelical Conservatism.* New York: W.W. Norton & Company, 2011.

Dormady, Jason H. *Primitive Revolution: Restorationist Religion and the Idea of the Mexican Revolution, 1940-1968.* Albuquerque, NM: University of New Mexico Press, 2011.

Driscoll, Mark, and Grace Driscoll. *Real Marriage: The*

Truth About Sex, Friendship, and Life Together. Nashville, TN: Thomas Nelson, 2012.

Dunaway, O.L. *The Key to Bible Understanding: Bible Questions and Answers From Bible Quotations or References To Where Answers May be Found*. 4th printing. O.L. Dunaway, 2008. First published 1954. http://literature.christadelphianresources.com/Dunaway /Key%20to%20Bible%20Understanding.pdf.

Enroth, Ronald. *Recovering from Churches That Abuse*. Grand Rapids, MI: Zondervan, 1994.

Evans, Rachel Held. *Searching for Sunday: Loving, Leaving, and Finding the Church*. Read by Rachel Held Evans. Nashville, TN: Nelson Books, 2015. MP3 audiobook, 7 hr., 28 min.

Eyre, Alan. *The Protesters*. Birmingham: The Christadelphian, 1975.

Fea, John. *Believe Me: The Evangelical Road to Donald Trump*. Grand Rapids, MI: William B. Eerdmans Publishing Company, 2018.

Fehrman, Craig. *Author in Chief: The Untold Story of Our Presidents and the Books They Wrote*. New York: Avid Reader Press, 2020.

Ferguson, Gordon. *Discipling: God's Plan to Train and Transform His People*. Woburn, MA: Discipleship Publications International, 1997.

———. *Prepared to Answer*. Woburn, MA: Discipleship Publications International, 1995.

Ferguson, Gordon and Wyndham Shaw. *Golden Rule Leadership: Building a Spirit of Team and Family in the Body of Christ*. Billerica, MA: Discipleship Publications International, 2001.

Fieser, James, ed. *Scottish Common Sense Philosophy:*

Sources and Origins. Vol. 5, *A Bibliography of Scottish Common Sense Philosophy*, edited by James Fieser. Bristol, England: Thoemmes Press, 2000.

Fischer, David Hackett. *Historians' Fallacies: Toward a Logic of Historical Thought*. New York: Harper & Row Publishers, Inc., 1970.

Flory, Richard W. and Donald E. Miller, eds. *GenX Religion*. New York: Routledge, 2000.

Foster, Douglas A. *A Life of Alexander Campbell*. Grand Rapids, MI: William B. Eerdmans Publishing Company, 2020.

———. *Will the Cycle Be Unbroken? Churches of Christ Face the 21st Century*. Abilene, TX: ACU Press, 1994.

Foster, Douglas A., Paul M. Blowers, Anthony L. Dunnavant, and D. Newell Williams, eds. *The Encyclopedia of the Stone-Campbell Movement*. Grand Rapids, MI: Wm. B. Eerdmans Publishing, 2004.

Frost, Michael. *Surprise the World! The Five Habits of Highly Missional People*. Colorado Springs, CO: NavPress, 2016.

Fudge, Edward, ed. *Resurrection! Essays in Honor of Homer Hailey*. Athens, AL: The C.E.I. Publishing Company, 1973.

———. *The Fire That Consumes: A Biblical and Historical Study of the Doctrine of Final Punishment*. 3rd ed. Eugene, OR: Cascade Books, 2011. Logos Bible Software.

Galbraith, Leslie R. and Heather F. Day. *The Disciples and American Culture: A Bibliography of Works by Disciples of Christ Members, 1866-1984*. Metuchen, NJ: The Scarecrow Press, 1990.

Galli, Mark. *God Wins: Heaven, Hell, and Why the Good*

News is Better than Love Wins. Carol Stream, IL: Tyndale House Publishers, 2011.

Gardner, Terry J. *The* Original *Gospel Guardian (1935-1936) and The Bible Banner (1938-1949) Indexed by Author and Subject, with A Biographical Sketch of the Life of Cled E. Wallace.* Indianapolis, IN: Terry Gardner, 1994.

Garrett, Margie H., ed. *Making a Difference: Florida College: The First Fifty Years.* Temple Terrace, FL: Florida College Bookstore, 1996.

Gentry, Ralph D. *A Critical Review of the Anti-Position on Church Cooperation and Orphan Homes.* Auburndale, FL: Orange Street Church of Christ, 1992.

Giambalvo, Carol and Herbert L. Rosedale, eds. *The Boston Movement: Critical Perspectives on the International Churches of Christ.* Bonita Springs, FL: American Family Foundation, 1996.

Gibbs, Eddie, and Ryan K. Bolger. *Emerging Churches: Creating Christian Community in Postmodern Cultures.* Grand Rapids, MI: Baker Academic, 2005.

Goff, Bob. *Love Does: Discover a Secretly Incredible Life in an Ordinary World.* Read by Bob Goff. Nashville, TN: Thomas Nelson, 2012. MP3 audiobook, 5 hr., 35 min.

Goodall, Charles G. *Evangelizing the 21st Century: Strategies for Bringing Souls to Christ Beyond the Pulpit.* Athens, AL: Truth Books, 2014.

Gorman, James L. *Among the Early Evangelicals: The Transatlantic Origins of the Stone Campbell Movement.* Abilene, TX: Abilene Christian University Press, 2017.

Grave, S.A. *The Scottish Philosophy of Common Sense.* Westport, CT: Greenwood Press, Inc., 1973. First published 1960 by Oxford University Press (New York).

Grizzell, Gary L. *Unscriptural Binding: A Current Debate About Saints Only Doctrine, Orphan Home Issue, Church Fellowship Meals*. Cookeville, TN: Pillars Publications, 1996.

Haight, Roger. *Christian Community in History, Volume I: Historical Ecclesiology*. New York: Continuum, 2004.

Hailey, Homer. *Attitudes and Consequences in the Restoration Movement*. 2nd ed. Rosemead, CA: The Old Paths Book Club, 1952.

———. *A Commentary on the Minor Prophets*. Grand Rapids, MI: Baker Book House Company, 1972.

———. *The Divorced and Remarried Who Come to God*. Rev. ed. Reno, NV: Nevada Publications, 1998.

———. *From Creation to the Day of Eternity: God's Great Plan for Man's Redemption*. Reno, NV: Nevada Publications, 1982.

———. *Hailey's Comments: A Compilation of Articles and Writings, Volume One*. Edited by Stanley W. Paher. Las Vegas, NV: Nevada Publications, 1985.

———. *Let's Go Fishing for Men*. 2nd ed. Abilene, TX: Chronicle Publishing Co., 1953.

———. *Revelation: An Introduction and Commentary*. Grand Rapids, MI: Baker Book House, 1979.

Halbwachs, Maurice. *On Collective Memory*. Edited and translated by Lewis A. Coser. Chicago: University of Chicago Press, 1992.

Harding, Ronald C. Jr. *The Chronicles of Modern-Day Christianity: The Evangelization of the Nations in This Generation*. Columbia, SC: SoldOut Press International, 2018.

Harper, Brad and Paul Louis Metzger. *Exploring Ecclesiology: An Evangelical and Ecumenical Introduction*. Grand Rapids, MI: Brazos Press, 2009.

Harper, Keith, ed. *Through a Glass Darkly: Contested Notions of Baptist Identity*. Tuscaloosa, AL: The University of Alabama Press, 2012.

Harper-Tant Debate: Abilene, Texas, November 27-30, 1955, between E.R. Harper, Abilene, Texas, and Fanning Yater Tant, Lufkin, Texas. Abilene, TX: Chronicle Publishing Company, Inc., 1956.

Harrell, David Edwin Jr. *The Churches of Christ in the Twentieth Century: Homer Hailey's Personal Journey of Faith*. Tuscaloosa, AL: The University of Alabama Press, 2000.

———. *Emergence of the "Church of Christ" Denomination*. Athens, AL: CEI Bookstore, n.d.

———. *A Social History of the Disciples of Christ*. 2 vols. Tuscaloosa, AL: The University of Alabama Press, 2003. First published 1966-73 by Disciples of Christ Historical Society (Nashville, TN).

Hatch, Nathan O. *The Democratization of American Christianity*. New Haven, CT: Yale University Press, 1989.

Hawkins, Ralph K. *A Heritage in Crisis: Where We've Been, Where We Are, and Where We're Going in Churches of Christ*. Paperback ed. Lanham, MD: University Press of America, Inc., 2008.

Heaster, Duncan. *Bible Basics: A Study Manual: Revealing the Joy and Peace of True Christianity*. Library ed. South Croydon, Surrey: Christadelphian Advancement Trust, 2001.

Hempton, David. *Methodism: Empire of the Spirit*. New Haven, CT: Yale University Press, 2005.

Hexham, Irving, Stephen Rost, and John W. Morehead II, eds. *Encountering New Religious Movements: A Holistic Evangelical Approach*. Grand Rapids, MI: Kregel Publications, 2004.

Hill, Samuel S. *One Name but Several Faces: Variety in*

Popular Christian Denominations in Southern History. Athens, GA: The University of Georgia Press, 1996.

Hill, Samuel S. and Charles H. Lippy, eds. *Encyclopedia of Religion in the South*. 2nd ed. Macon, GA: Mercer University Press, 2005.

Hirsch, Alan. *The Forgotten Ways: Reactivating the Missional Church*. Grand Rapids, MI: Brazos Press, 2006.

Hodge, Frederick Arthur. *The Plea and the Pioneers in Virginia: A History of the Rise and Early Progress of the Disciples of Christ in Virginia, with Biographical Sketches of the Pioneer-Preachers*. Richmond, VA: Everett Waddey Company, 1905. https://archive.org/details/pleapioneersinviooinhodg.

Hofstadter, Douglas R. *Gödel, Escher, Bach: An Eternal Golden Braid*. Twentieth anniversary ed. New York: Basic Books, 1999.

Holloway, Gary. *Saints, Demons, and Asses: Southern Preacher Anecdotes*. Bloomington, IN: Indiana University Press, 1989.

Holloway, Gary and Douglas A. Foster. *Renewing God's People: A Concise History of Churches of Christ*. Abilene, TX: ACU Press, 2006.

Hooper, Robert E. *A Distinct People: A History of the Churches of Christ in the 20th Century*. Eugene, OR: Wipf and Stock Publishers, 2001.

Hughes, Richard T. *Christian America and the Kingdom of God*. Urbana, IL: University of Illinois Press, 2009.

———. *Reviving the Ancient Faith: The Story of Churches of Christ in America*. Grand Rapids, MI: William B. Eerdmans Publishing Company, 1996.

———, ed. *The American Quest for the Primitive Church*. Urbana, IL: University of Illinois Press, 1988.

———, ed. *The Primitive Church in the Modern World.* Urbana, IL: University of Illinois Press, 1995.

Hughes, Richard T. and C. Leonard Allen. *Illusions of Innocence: Protestant Primitivism in America, 1630-1875.* With a foreword by Robert N. Bellah. Chicago, IL: The University of Chicago Press, 1988.

Hyndman, Rob J. *Learn to Read the Bible Effectively: Sponsored by the Christadelphians.* NIV edition. Beechworth, Victoria, Australia: Bethel Publications, 1998. http://thechristadelphians.org/btcd/downloads/lrbe.pdf.

Illinois Senate Education Committee. *Cult Activities on College Campuses.* Springfield, IL, 1994.

Jacoby, Douglas. *Shining Like Stars: An Evangelism Handbook.* 4th ed. Newton Upper Falls, MA: Illumination Publishers International, 2006.

———. *The Powerful Delusion: How to Study with Charismatics.* 2nd ed. London: London Church of Christ, 1988.

———. *The Spirit: The Work of the Holy Spirit in the Lives of Disciples.* Rev. ed. Newton Upper Falls, MA: Illumination Publishers International, 2005.

———, ed. *Advanced Christian Training.* London: Central London Church of Christ, 1986.

Jannaway, Frank G. *Christadelphian Answers on All Kinds of Difficulties, Objections, Arguments, and Questions, Exhibiting "The Truth" in Opposition to the Dogmas of Papal and Protestant Christendom.* Houston, TX: The Herald Press, n.d. http://www.antipas.org/pdf_files/christadelphian_answers.pdf.

———, ed. *Christadelphian Treasury: Forming a Collection of Extracts from Writings Exhibiting "The Truth" in Opposition to the Dogmas of Papal and Protestant Christendom by Dr. John*

Thomas, Robert Roberts, and Other Well-Known Christadelphians. Houston, TX: The Herald Press, n.d.

Jenkins, Ferrell. *The Early Church: First Century Christianity as revealed in the New Testament*. Temple Terrace, FL: Florida College Bookstore, 1999.

———, ed. *A Tribute to Melvin D. Curry, Jr.* Temple Terrace, FL: Florida College Bookstore, 1997.

Jenkins, Kathleen E. *Awesome Families: The Promise of Healing Relationships in the International Churches of Christ*. New Brunswick, NJ: Rutgers University Press, 2005.

Jennings, Alvin. *How Christianity Grows in the City*. Fort Worth, TX: Star Bible Publications, 1985.

———, ed. *Introducing the Church of Christ: Distinctive Features of the Church of Christ Discussed By Over Fifty of Her Ministers*. Fort Worth, TX: Star Bible Publications, 1981.

Jones, Jerry. *Back to the Basics*. Bridgeton, MO: Mid-America Book and Tape Sales, 1988.

———. *Discipleship in God's Eternal Purpose: A Biblical Study of the Design, Demand, and Demonstration of Being a Disciple of Jesus Christ*. Searcy, AR: Jerry Jones, 1984.

———. *What Does the Boston Movement Teach?* 3 vols. Bridgeton, MO: Mid-America Book and Tape Sales, 1990.

Jones, Thomas A. *In Search of a City: An Autobiographical Perspective on a Remarkable but Controversial Movement*. Spring Hill, TN: DPI Books, 2007.

———. *Letters to New Disciples: Practical Advice for Those Who Have Decided to Follow Jesus*. 2nd ed. Spring Hill, TN: Discipleship Publications International, 2007.

———. *Mind Change: The Overcomer's Handbook*. Woburn, MA: Discipleship Publications International, 1994.

Jones, Thomas and Sheila Jones, eds. *Glory in the Church:*

Powerful Readings Exploring the Eternal Plan for the Family of God. Woburn, MA: Discipleship Publications International, 1996.

Kelly, Norm. *Directions in Australian Electoral Reform: Professionalism and Partisanship in Electoral Management*. Canberra, Australia: ANU Press, 2012.

Key, Barclay. *Race & Restoration: Churches of Christ and the Black Freedom Struggle*. Baton Rouge, LA: Louisiana State University Press, 2020.

Kimball, Dan. *The Emerging Church: Vintage Christianity for New Generations*. Grand Rapids,MI: Zondervan, 2003.

———. *Emerging Worship: Creating New Worship Gatherings for Emerging Generations*. Grand Rapids, MI: Zondervan, 2004.

Lemmon, Richard. *Faith and Baptism: Illustrated From the Bible*. Baltimore, MD: SamuelSands, 1841. http://christadelphianbooks.org/books.html.

Lewis, Warren and Hans Rollman, eds. *Restoring the First-century Church in the Twenty-first Century: Essays on the Stone-Campbell Restoration Movement in Honor of Don Haymes*. Eugene, OR: Wipf and Stock Publishers, 2005.

Lippy, Charles H. *The Christadelphians in North America*. Lewiston, NY: The Edwin Mellen Press, 1989.

Long, Loretta M. *The Life of Selina Campbell: A Fellow Soldier in the Cause of Restoration*. Tuscaloosa, AL: The University of Alabama Press, 2001.

Love, Mark, Douglas A. Foster, and Randall J. Harris. *Seeking a Lasting City: The Church's Journey in the Story of God*. Abilene, TX: ACU Press, 2005.

Mansfield, H.P. *Guidebook to the New Testament*. West

Beach, South Australia: Logos Publications,1983. http://christadelphianbooks.org/books.html.

———. *In Defence of the Faith*. West Beach, South Australia: Logos Publications, n.d. http://christadelphianbooks.org/books.html.

———. *Key to the Understanding of the Scriptures*. Findon, South Australia: Logos Publications, n.d. http://christadelphianbooks.org/books.html.

Marti, Gerardo and Gladys Ganiel. *The Deconstructed Church: Understanding Emerging Christianity*. New York: Oxford University Press, 2014.

Martin, F.H. (Buddy). *Multiplying Ministries Movement: A Six-Part Informative Lecture Series*. Houston, TX: Memorial Church of Christ, 1987.

Mason, Ra. *Japan's Relations with North Korea and the Recalibration of Risk*. New York: Routledge, 2014.

McClish, Dub. "The Crossroads/Boston Movement." In *God Hath Spoken: The Tenth Annual Southwest Lectures*, edited by Bill Jackson, 314–329. Austin, TX: Southwest Publications, 1991.

McGreevy, John T. "American Religion." In *American History Now*, edited by Eric Foner and Lisa McGirr, 242–260. Philadelphia: Temple University Press, 2011.

McHaffie, Ruth. *Brethren Indeed?: Christadelphians and "Outsiders" (16th–21st Century)*. Ian McHaffie, 2001. http://www.christadelphianbooks.org/books.html.

McKnight, Scot. *The Blue Parakeet: Rethinking How You Read the Bible*. Grand Rapids, MI: Zondervan, 2008.

———. *Fasting*. Nashville, TN: Thomas Nelson, 2009.

———. *The Jesus Creed: Loving God, Loving Others*. Brewster, MA: Paraclete Press, 2004.

McLaren, Brian D. *Everything Must Change: Jesus, Global Crises, and a Revolution of Hope*. Nashville, TN: Thomas Nelson, 2007.

———. *A Generous Orthodoxy: Why I am a Missional, Evangelical, Post/Protestant, Liberal/Conservative, Mystical/Poetic, Biblical, Charismatic/Contemplative, Fundamentalist/Calvinist, Anabaptist/Anglican, Methodist, Catholic, Green, Incarnational, Depressed-Yet-Hopeful, Emergent, Unfinished Christian*. Grand Rapids, MI: Zondervan, 2004.

———. *The Great Spiritual Migration: How the World's Largest Religion is Seeking a Better Way to be Christian*. New York: Convergent Books, 2016.

———. *A New Kind of Christian: A Tale of Two Friends on a Spiritual Journey*. San Francisco: Jossey-Bass, 2001.

———. *A New Kind of Christianity: Ten Questions That are Transforming the Faith*. New York: HarperOne, 2010.

———. *The Secret Message of Jesus: Uncovering the Truth That Could Change Everything*. Nashville, TN: Thomas Nelson, Inc., 2006.

McLeod, Hugh. *Secularisation in Western Europe, 1848-1914*. New York: St. Martin's, 2000.

McManus, Erwin Raphael. *Soul Cravings: An Exploration of the Human Spirit*. Nashville, TN: Thomas Nelson, 2006.

Mead, Frank S., Samuel S. Hill, and Craig D. Atwood, eds. *Handbook of Denominations in the United States*. 12th ed. Nashville, TN: Abingdon Press, 2005.

Mead, Frank S., Samuel S. Hill, and Craig D. Atwood, eds. *Handbook of Denominations in the United States*. 13th ed. Nashville, TN: Abingdon Press, 2010.

Melton, J. Gordon. *Religious Bodies in the United States: A Directory*. Rev. ed. New York: Garland Publishing, 1992.

Meltzer, Mitchell. *Secular Revelations: The Constitution of the United States and Classic American Literature*. Cambridge, MA: Harvard University Press, 2005.

Meyer, Birgit and Peter Pels, eds. *Magic and Modernity: Interfaces of Revelation and Concealment*. Stanford, CA: Stanford University Press, 2003.

Meyers, Sharen. *Regaining Faith After Boston: An Insider's View*. Fort Worth, TX: Star Bible Publications, n.d.

Middleton, J. Richard and Brian J. Walsh. *Truth is Stranger Than It Used to Be: Biblical Faith in a Postmodern Age*. Downers Grove, IL: InterVarsity Press, 1995.

Miller, Donald. *Blue Like Jazz: Nonreligious Thoughts on Christian Spirituality*. Ltd. ed. Nashville, TN: Thomas Nelson, 2009.

———. *Building a Story Brand: Clarify Your Message So Customers Will Listen*. New York: HarperCollins Leadership, 2017.

———. *Father Fiction: Chapters for a Fatherless Generation*. New York: Howard Books, 2010.

———. *Jazz Notes: Improvisations on* Blue Like Jazz. Nashville, TN: Thomas Nelson, 2008.

———. *A Million Miles in a Thousand Years: How I Learned to Live a Better Story*. Nashville, TN: Thomas Nelson, 2009.

———. *Scary Close: Dropping the Act and Finding True Intimacy*. Nashville, TN: Nelson Books, 2014.

———. *Searching For God Knows What*. Exp. ed. Nashville, TN: Thomas Nelson, 2010.

———. *Through Painted Deserts: Light, God, and Beauty on the Open Road*. Nashville, TN: Thomas Nelson, 2005.

Miller, Steven P. *The Age of Evangelicalism: America's Born-Again Years*. New York: Oxford University Press, 2014.

Miller, Timothy, ed. *America's Alternative Religions*. Albany, NY: State University of New York Press, 1995.

Mirowski, Philip. *Science-Mart: Privatizing American Science*. Cambridge, MA: Harvard University Press, 2011.

———. *The Effortless Economy of Science?* Durham, NC: Duke University Press, 2004.

Mulligan, Mary Alice, ed. *The Living Pulpit: Sermons That Illustrate Preaching in the Stone-Campbell Movement, 1968-2018*. St. Louis, MO: CBP, 2018.

Music, Goebel. *Behold the Pattern*. Colleyville, TX: Goebel Music Publications, 1991.

Nelson, Robert. *Understanding the Crossroads Controversy*. Gainesville, FL: published by the author, 1981.

Nichols, Ryan and Gideon Yaffe. "Thomas Reid." In *The Stanford Encyclopedia of Philosophy*, Winter 2016 ed., edited by Edward N. Zalta. https://plato.stanford.edu/archives/win2016/entries/reid/.

Noll, Mark A. *The Scandal of the Evangelical Mind*. Grand Rapids, MI: Wm. B. Eerdmans Publishing Co., 1994.

Norrie, William. *The Early History of the Gospel of the Kingdom of God in Britain with Historical, Critical, and Social Reminiscences of Persons, Places, and Events, Volume I*. Earlston, Berwickshire: The Waverley Press, 1904. http://www.christadelphianresearch.com/theearlyhistory-norrie.htm.

Novick, Peter. *That Noble Dream: The "Objectivity Question" and the American Historical Profession*. New York: Cambridge University Press, 1998.

Odifreddi, Piergiorgio. *Classical Recursion Theory: The Theory of Functions and Sets of Natural Numbers*. New York: Elsevier Science Publishing Company, Inc., 1989.

Olbricht, Thomas H. *Reflection on My Life: In the Kingdom and the Academy*. Eugene, OR: Wipf & Stock, 2012.

One Hundred Years of The Christadelphian: A Centenary Review of the Magazine and the Community, July, 1864, to July, 1964. Birmingham: The Christadelphian, 1964.

Ormerod, Neil. *Re-Visioning the Church: An Experiment in Systematic-Historical Ecclesiology*. Minneapolis, MN: Fortress Press, 2014.

Owens, Marion D. *Time to Go: A New Look at the Boston Movement*. Fort Worth, TX: Star Bible Publications, n.d.

Pagitt, Doug. *Church Re-Imagined: The Spiritual Formation of People in Communities of Faith*. Grand Rapids, MI: Zondervan, 2005.

Pagitt, Doug, and Tony Jones, eds. *An Emergent Manifesto of Hope*. Grand Rapids, MI: Baker Books, 2007.

Paton, Alan. *Cry, the Beloved Country*. New York: Charles Scribner's Sons, 1950. First published 1948.

———. *Too Late the Phalarope*. New York: Charles Scribner's Sons, 1953.

Patterson, Noble and Terry J. Gardner, eds. *Foy E. Wallace, Jr.: Soldier of the Cross*. Fort Worth, TX: Wallace Memorial Fund, 1999.

Patton, Herschel. *The Bible Story and Sixty-Five Years of Telling It*. Temple Terrace, FL: Florida College, 2006.

Planet Earth: Will God's Kingdom Be Set Up Here? A Debate on a Hot Subject. Fort Worth, TX: Star Bible & Tract Corp., 1974.

Roberts, Robert. *Christendom Astray: or, Popular Christianity (Both in Faith and Practice), Shewn to be Unscriptural; and the True Nature of the Ancient Apostolic Faith Exhibited in Eighteen Lectures*. Birmingham: R. Roberts, 1897.

———. *Dr. Thomas: His Life and Work: A Biography Illustrative of the Process by which the System of Truth Revealed in the Bible has been Extricated in Modern Times from the Obscuration of Romish and Protestant Traditions*. Birmingham: C.C. Walker, 1911.

———. *A Three Nights' Discussion Between Mr. Robert Roberts, Editor of the 'Christadelphian,' and Mr. Louis Stern, An Orthodox Jew, of Birmingham, in the Temperance Hall, Birmingham, On Tuesday, Wednesday, & Thursday, October 17th, 18th, & 19th, 1871. Rev. B. Wright, Unitarian Minister, in the Chair.* Houston, TX: Herald Press, n.d.

———. *The Truth in the Nineteenth Century: or the Lessons of Thirty Years' Experience Presented in the Form of a Guide to the Formation and Conduct of Ecclesias, in the Characteristic Circumstances of an Age when the Truth as Apostolically Delivered has been Revived in the Ways of Divine Providence, Without the Co-Operation and Living Guidance of the Holy Spirit as Enjoyed in the Apostolic Age*. Birmingham: Robert Roberts, 1883. http://www. antipas.org/pdf_files/ e_g_1883.pdf.

Robinson, Edward J. *Hard-Fighting Soldiers: A History of African American Churches of Christ*. Knoxville, TN: University of Tennessee Press, 2019.

———. *Show Us How You Do It: Marshall Keeble and the Rise of Black Churches of Christ in the United States, 1914-1968.* Tuscaloosa, AL: The University of Alabama Press, 2008.

Roeper, Tom and Margaret Speas, eds. *Recursion: Complexity in Cognition*. Cham, Switzerland: Springer International Publishing Switzerland, 2014.

Rosenzweig, Roy and David Thelen. *The Presence of the Past: Popular Uses of History in American Life*. New York: Columbia University Press, 2000.

Royster, Carl H., comp. *Churches of Christ in the United States.* 2015 ed. Nashville: 21st Century Christian, 2015.

Schillebeeckx, Edward. *The Church with a Human Face: A New and Expanded Theology of Ministry*. Translated by John Bowden. New York: The Crossroad Publishing Company, 1985.

Sisman, Keith. *Traces of the Kingdom: One Thousand Years of the Churches of Christ in England.* 2nd ed. Ramsey, UK: Forbidden Books, 2010.

Smith, Christian with Melinda Lundquist Denton. *Soul Searching: The Religious and Spiritual Lives of American Teenagers*. New York: Oxford University Press, 2005.

Smith, F. LaGard. *Radical Restoration: A Call for Pure and Simple Christianity*. Nashville, TN: Cotswold Publishing, 2001.

Smith, James K.A. *Who's Afraid of Postmodernism? Taking Derrida, Lyotard, and Foucault to Church*. Grand Rapids, MI: Baker Academic, 2006.

Stanback, C. Foster. *Into All Nations: A History of the International Churches of Christ*. Newton Upper Falls, MA: Illumination Publishers International, 2005.

Stearsman, Jackie M. *A Critique of the Multiplying Ministries of the Boston Church of Christ*. Lakeland, Florida: Stearsman's Publications, 1987.

Stephens, Randall J. *The Fire Spreads: Holiness and Pentecostalism in the American South*. Cambridge, MA: Harvard University Press, 2008.

Stevens-Beevers Debate on the New Testament and Roman Catholicism: A Public Discussion Between Eldred Stevens and Eric Beevers, Ph.D. Nashville, TN: Eldred Stevens, 1952.

Stewart, Kenneth J. *In Search of Ancient Roots: The Chris-*

tian Past and the Evangelical Identity Crisis. Downers Grove, IL: IVP Academic, 2017.

Sutcliffe, R. *The Trinity Hurdle: Engaging Christadelphians, Arians, and Unitarians with the Gospel of the Triune God*. Eugene, OR: Wipf & Stock, 2016.

Sweet, Leonard. *The Gospel According to Starbucks: Living with a Grande Passion*. Colorado Springs, CO: WaterBrook Press, 2007.

———. *Nudge: Awakening Each Other to the God Who's Already There*. Read by Dean Gallagher. Colorado Springs, CO: David C. Cook, 2010. MP3 audiobook, 9 hr., 14 min.

———. *Soul Tsunami: Sink or Swim in New Millennium Culture*. Grand Rapids, MI: Zondervan Publishing House, 1999.

Taliaferro, Mike. *The Lion Never Sleeps: Preparing Those You Love for Satan's Attacks*. Spring, TX: Illumination Publishers, 2014.

Tant, Fanning Yater. *J.D. Tant – Texas Preacher: A Biography*. Erlanger, KY: Faith and Facts Press, 1958.

———. *Nannie Yater Tant – Reminiscences of a Pioneer Preacher's Wife*. Indianapolis, IN: Faith and Facts Press, 1990.

———. *"How New Testament Churches Can, and Can Not, Cooperate: or, What Is Wrong with Herald of Truth?" A Study of "Sponsoring Church" Cooperation."*

Tennant, Harry. *The Christadelphians: What They Believe and Preach*. Birmingham, UK: The Christadelphian, 1988. First published 1986 by The Christadelphian (Birmingham, UK).

Thomas, John. *Elpis Israel: Being an Exposition of the Kingdom of God; with Reference to the Time of the End, and the*

Age to Come. 4th ed. West Hoboken, NJ: published by the author, 1867.

———. *Eureka: An Exposition of the Apocalypse in Harmony with "the Things of the Kingdom of the Deity and the Name of Jesus Anointed," Volume 1*. West Beach, South Australia: Logos Publications, n.d.

Tickle, Phyllis. *Emergence Christianity: What It Is, Where It Is Going, and Why It Matters*. Grand Rapids, MI: Baker Books, 2012.

———. *The Great Emergence: How Christianity is Changing and Why*. Grand Rapids, MI: Baker Books, 2008.

Townsend, J.C. *A History of Churches of Christ in Florida with Other Related Stories, 1869–1949*. Compiled by Geraldine McLeod Thompson. Florida Bible Camp, 2003.

The Truth Vindicated: The Lee-Mansfield Debates, February 1962 with Scriptural Index. Brisbane, Australia: Graphomatic Press, n.d.

Treier, Daniel J. and Walter A. Elwell, eds. *Evangelical Dictionary of Theology*. 3rd ed. Grand Rapids, MI: Baker Academic, 2017.

Tristano, Richard M. *The Origins of the Restoration Movement: An Intellectual History*. Atlanta, GA: Glenmary Research Center, 1988.

Turner, John G. *Bill Bright & Campus Crusade for Christ: The Renewal of Evangelicalism in Postwar America*. Chapel Hill, NC: The University of North Carolina Press, 2008.

———. *The Mormon Jesus: A Biography*. Cambridge, MA: Belknap Press, 2016.

Ullman, John. *The First Principles of the One True Faith: Set Forth in a Series of Studies*. Findon, Australia: Logos Publications, n.d. http://christadelphianbooks.org/books.html.

Waddey, John. *Back to the Fountain-Head: Studies on the Restoration of New Testament Christianity*. Delight, AR: Gospel Light Publishing Co., 2010.

———. *Lawmakers and Judges: Studies in the Doctrines and Practices of "NonInstitutional" Churches of Christ and Their Teachers*. Sun City West, AZ: John Waddey, n.d.

Waldrep, B. Dwain and Scott Billingsley, eds. *Recovering the Margins of American Religious History: The Legacy of David Edwin Harrell Jr.* Tuscaloosa, AL: The University of Alabama Press, 2012.

Wallace, Foy E. Jr. *The Certified Gospel: A Series of Sermons Preached at the 6th Street Church of Christ in Port Arthur, Texas, October 26th through November 10th, 1937*. 2nd ed. Lufkin, TX: Roy E. Cogdill Publishing Company, 1948.

——— *The Current Issues*. Nashville, TN: Foy E. Wallace, Jr., Publications, 1967.

Watt, David Harrington. *Bible-Carrying Christians: Conservative Protestants and Social Power*. New York: Oxford University Press, 2002.

Webber, Robert E. *Ancient-Future Faith: Rethinking Evangelicalism for a Postmodern World*. Grand Rapids, MI: Baker Books, 1999.

———. *Evangelicals on the Canterbury Trail: Why Evangelicals Are Attracted to the Liturgical Church*. Waco, TX: Word Books, 1985.

———. *The Church in the World: Opposition, Tension, or Transformation?* Grand Rapids, MI: Academie Books, 1986.

Werner, Julia Stewart. *The Primitive Methodist Connexion: Its Background and Early History*. Madison, WI: The University of Wisconsin Press, 1984.

West, Earl Irvin. *The Search for the Ancient Order: A History of the Restoration Movement*. 4 vols. Germantown, TN: Religious Book Service, 1949–87.

West, Earl Irvin. *Searcher for the Ancient Order: The Golden Odyssey of Earl I. West*. Nashville, TN: Gospel Advocate Company, 2004.

Wharton, Edward C. *The Church of Christ: A Presentation of the Distinctive Nature and Identity of the New Testament Church*. West Monroe, LA: Howard Book House, 1987.

Wiener, Jon. *Historians in Trouble: Plagiarism, Fraud, and Politics in the Ivory Tower*. New York: New Press, 2005.

Williams, D. Newell, Douglas A. Foster, and Paul M. Blowers, eds. *The Stone-Campbell Movement: A Global History*. St. Louis: Chalice Press, 2013.

Williams, Daniel K. *Defenders of the Unborn: The Pro-Life Movement Before* Roe v. Wade. New York: Oxford University Press, 2016.

———. *God's Own Party: The Making of the Christian Right*. New York: Oxford University Press, 2010.

Wilson, Andrew R. *The History of the Christadelphians, 1864-1885: The Emergence of a Denomination*. Australia Square, NSW: Shalom Publications, 1997.

Wilson, Bryan R. *Sects and Society: A Sociological Study of Three Religious Groups in Britain*. Westport, CT: Greenwood Press, Inc., 1978. First published 1961 by W. Heinemann (London).

Wright, N.T. *Revelation for Everyone*. Louisville, KY: Westminster John Knox Press, 2011.

Wright, Ben and Zachary W. Dresser, eds. *Apocalypse and the Millennium in the American Civil War Era*. Baton Rouge, LA: Louisiana State University Press, 2013.

Yeakley, Flavil R. Jr. *Why They Left: Listening to Those*

Who Have Left Churches of Christ. Nashville, TN: Gospel Advocate Company, 2012.

———, ed. *The Discipling Dilemma: A Study of the Discipling Movement Among Churches of Christ*. Nashville, TN: Gospel Advocate Company, 1988.

Dissertations/Theses

Baker, Barry Dean. "A Critical Analysis of the Theory and Practice of Preaching in the Emerging Church Movement." PhD diss., Mid-America Baptist Theological Seminary, 2006.

Blench, David. "Appreciative Inquiry as a Resource for Positive Change in a Church Ministry." MS thesis, Pepperdine University, 2017.

Bybee, Jason. "Developing an Intentional Mentoring Model for Disciple Formation at the Mayfair Church of Christ." DMin thesis, Abilene Christian University, 2014.

Cannon, Robert L. "The British Government and the War Resisters During World War One: A Study in Confrontation and Compromise." MA thesis, California State University Dominguez Hills, 1999.

Cates, Carl M. "Cult Rhetoric: A Genre of Manipulative Speech." PhD diss., Florida State University, 1994.

Chia, Lloyd. "Emerging Faith Boundaries: Bridge-Building, Inclusion, and the Emerging Church Movement in America." PhD diss., University of Missouri-Columbia, 2010.

Cooley, Luann C. "Discipling Sisters: How Women Learn the Culture of a Conservative Christian Church." PhD diss., The University of Georgia, 2006.

Cox, Brady Kal. "Postwar Churches of Christ Mission

Work: The Philippines as a Case Study."MA thesis, Abilene Christian University, 2018.

Duncan, John Alan. "A Critical Analysis of Preaching in the Emerging Church." PhD diss.,Southern Baptist Theological Seminary, 2011.

Gaw, Jerry Lewis. "A History of Churches of Christ in the United Kingdom to 1867." MA thesis, Northwestern State University of Louisiana, 1983.

Gillams, Sheila Hope. "Principle and Practice: The Quandary of African American Restorationists in the History and Theology of the Church of Christ, Disciples of Christ, 1850-1950." PhD diss., Union Theological Seminary, 2002.

Hall, Douglas Leon. "Authoritarian Theology in the Boston Church of Christ: A Short-Circuit of Christianity." MA thesis, Abilene Christian University, 1991.

Hardin, John C. "Common Cause: B.C. Goodpasture, the *Gospel Advocate*, and Churches of Christ in the Twentieth Century." PhD diss., Auburn University, 2009.

Harshbarger, Randy. "A History of the Institutional Controversy Among Texas Churches of Christ: 1945 to the Present." MA thesis, Stephen F. Austin State University, 2007.

Hendricks, Roger D. "The Development of the International Churches of Christ." MTS thesis, Christian Theological Seminary, 1997.

Henegar, Richard J. "Discipling Churches of Christ: An Assessment of Pre, Peak, and Post Involvement of Former Members Using the Myers-Briggs Type Indicator." PhD diss., United States International University, 1992.

Jacoby, Douglas Anderson. "Equipping the Members:

Organizing an Effective Congregational Teaching Day and Follow-On Program." DMin project, Drew University, 1999.

Jones, Michael Melborn. "The Hermeneutical Controversy in the Churches of Christ and Implications for Preaching Within That Tradition." PhD diss., Southern Baptist Theological Seminary, 1995.

Kinnard, G. Steve. "New Wineskins: Formation of a Ministry of Multimedia Education Integrating the Bible, Geography, and Archaeology." DMin project, Drew University, 1999.

Kim, Woo Joon. "An Evangelical Critique of the Emergent Church's Hermeneutics and Its Effects on Theology, Message, and Method of Evangelism." PhD diss., Southwestern Baptist Theological Seminary, 2012.

Lappeman, James. "Factors Influencing The International Church of Christ's Decision Not To Require Formal Theological Training For Its Ministers From 1979-2002." MA thesis, University of Cape Town, 2014.

Major, James Brooks. "The Role of Periodicals in the Development of the Disciples of Christ, 1850-1910." PhD diss., Vanderbilt University, 1966.

McCauley, Morris Lynn. "Freed-Hardeman College Lectures, 1969-1970: Rhetoric of Reaction." MA thesis, Louisiana State University, 1972.

Moorhouse, William Mervin. "The Restoration Movement: The Rhetoric of Jacksonian Restorationism in a Frontier Religion." PhD diss., Indiana University, 1968.

Packard, Josh. "Organizational Structure, Religious Belief, and Resistance: The Emerging Church." PhD diss., Vanderbilt University, 2008.

Paden, Russell R. "From the Churches of Christ to the

Boston Movement: A Comparative Study." MA thesis, University of Kansas, 1994.

Petter, Ron. "The Role of the Restoration Hermeneutic in the Fractures of the Churches of Christin the Twentieth Century." MTS thesis, McMaster Divinity College, 2009.

Phillips, Myer. "A Historical Study of the Attitude of the Churches of Christ toward Other Denominations." PhD diss., Baylor University, 1983.

Pope, Jesse Curtis. "The Restoration Ideal in American Religious Thought." PhD diss., Florida State University, 1990.

Simcox, Kate D. "Performing Postmodern Christian: Communication in the Emerging Church and the Renegotiation of Divine Knowledge." PhD diss., Bowling Green State University, 2005.

Snyder, Lewis Leroy. "Alexander Campbell as a Change Agent within the Stone-Campbell Movement from 1830-1840." PhD diss., Ohio State University, 1987.

Sockwell, Stuart Davis. "The 'Pastor System Debate' within the Churches of Christ: An Argumentative Analysis Using a Fields Approach." MA thesis, University of Alabama, 1990.

St Clair, Gary Lynn. "A Historical Research Study of The Boston Movement." MS thesis, Concordia University Wisconsin, 2000.

Steele, Terrance S. "The Missiology of the Emerging Church in Portland, Oregon." PhD diss., Trinity Evangelical Divinity School, 2012.

Stockdale, Todd J. "Ecclesiological Contributions of Emerging Churches for Their Parent Communities." PhD thesis, The University of Edinburgh, 2013.

Thompson, William Lester. "A Study of the Theology of

Dr. John Thomas, Founder of the Christadelphians." MAR thesis, Butler University, 1946.

Whitesel, Robert B. "Recurring Patterns of Organic Churches: An Analysis of Twelve Emerging Congregations." PhD diss., Fuller Theological Seminary, 2009.

Winrow, Dewayne. "A Social Ethical Analysis of the Restoration Motif of Churches of Christ." PhD diss., University of Southern California, 2000.

Wiseman, Karyn L. "Grace Space: The Creation of Worship Space for the Postmodern/Emerging Church." PhD diss., Drew University, 2006.

Wolfgang, James Stephen. "Fundamentalism and the Churches of Christ, 1910-1930." MA thesis, Vanderbilt University, 1990.

———. "Science and Religion Issues in the American Restoration Movement." PhD diss., University of Kentucky, 1997.

Wooten, Martin Edward. "The Boston Movement as a 'Revitalization Movement.'" DMin thesis, Harding Graduate School of Religion, 1990.

Wright, James H. "Discerning the Path of Christian Child Care: Trends in Funding Sources, Program Offerings, and Spiritual Activities." DMin diss., Southern Christian University, 2000.

Wyble, Erin Theresa. "Telling Stories: Applying Feminist Writing Strategies to 'Emerging Church' Theologies." PhD thesis, Pennsylvania State University, 2006.

Yi, Joseph Eugene. "God and Karate in the Southside: American Culture and Civic Participation in a Global Era, Volume One." PhD diss., The University of Chicago, 2004.

Zenor, Charles Wesley. "A History of Biblical Interpretation in the Church of Christ: 1901–1976." ThD diss., Iliff School of Theology, 1976.

Zukeran, Patrick Y. "A Critique of the International Church of Christ." ThM thesis, Dallas Theological Seminary, 1996.

Films

Hoover, Steve, dir. *Blood Brother*. 2013; Pittsburgh, PA: Animal Media Group, 2013. Tubi.

Wood, Jeff, dir. *Hell and Mr. Fudge*. 2012; Toronto, ON: Phase 4 Films, 2013. Tubi.

Musical Recordings

Christadelphian Art Trust. *Songs in a Strange Land*. Christadelphian Art Trust, 2004, Spotify.

Handsworth Christadelphians. *Voice of His Word*. Handsworth Christadelphians, 2015, Spotify.

The Liturgists. *Garden*. The Liturgists, 2014, Spotify.

The Liturgists. *God Our Mother*. The Liturgists, 2014, Spotify.

Pamphlets

Abel, Ron. *"Let Her be Covered…": The Hats of Christadelphian Sisters: a Biblical Consideration*. Vernon, British Columbia: Wayside Press Ltd., n.d.http://christadelphianbooks.org/ books.html.

Bible Q&A. Hyderabad, India: Printland Publishers, 2001.http://www.christadelphia.org/pamphlet/p_bibleqa.pdf.

Bull, Michael N. *The Life of a True Christian*. Hyderabad, India: Printland Publishers, n.d. http://www.christadelphia.org/ pamphlet/p_christian.pdf.

———. *The Bible—The Word of God*. Hyderabad, India: Printland Publishers, n.d. http://www.christadelphia.org/pamphlet/p_bible.pdf.

Ferguson, Gordon. *The Crossroads Controversy: One Preacher's Perspective*. Fort Worth, TX: Star Bible & Tract Corp., 1983.

First Forty Days Quiet Times Series. http://www.hampton-roadschurch.com/new-christians-studies.

Harding School of Theology. *Periodicals Associated with the Churches of Christ*, January 2008. https://hst.edu/wp-content/uploads/2017/04/PERIODICALS-ASSOCIATED-WITH-THE-CHURCHES-OF-CHRIST.pdf

Jacoby, Doug. *Statistics and Church Growth*. 2000. https://www.douglasjacoby.com/wp-content/uploads/Stats-Final.pdf.

Jenkins, Ferrell. "Please Don't Call Us 'Anti' (An Update on the Non-Institutional Churches of Christ)." Lecture presented at the 55th Anniversary Pepperdine University BibleLectures, Malibu, CA, May 1, 1998.

Lively Stones Collective. *Survey Report: Your Relationship with Our Community*. http://www.livelystonescollective.-com/lively-stones-surveys/.

McKean, Kip. *First Principles*. Discipleship Media, LLC, 2009. http://www.caicc.net/wp-content/uploads/2012/03/First Principles_Eng.pdf.

Performances

Johnson, Steven Leslie and E. Sherwin Mackintosh. *Upside Down: A Musical Tale After the Christ*. The Upside Down Theatre Company. Performed 2016. St. Louis, MO. https://www.youtube.com/watch?v=vQW3bNuU-y4.

Periodicals

Apostolic Advocate

Auburn Beacon

Bible Banner

Bible Magazine

Biblical Discipleship Quarterly

Boston Bulletin

Campus Journal

Chicago Fire

Christadelphian Advocate

Christadelphian eJournal of Biblical Interpretation

Christadelphian Tidings Magazine

Christian Chronicle

Christian Informer

Christianity Today

Glad Tidings of the Kingdom of God

Gospel Banner and Millennial Advocate

Gospel Guardian

Herald of the Kingdom and Age to Come

LA Story

Sanctuary-Keeper

Spiritual Sword

Testimony

Think On These Things

Truth Magazine

Watchman Magazine

Young Worker's Advocate and Mutual Magazine

Podcasts

Building a Story Brand with Donald Miller

Christadelphian Carelinks Bible Talks

Florida College Chapel
ICOC Weekly Podcast
The Robcast
Tick, Talk, Take with Doug Pagitt

Unpublished Sources

Bates, Graham. "Removing the Bridge Keeper: Comparing the Pioneer Restoration Movement to the Pioneer Emerging Church Movement." Unpublished manuscript, last modified July 4, 2014. Microsoft Word file.

Dannemiller, Sarah. "Power in Submission: An Analysis of Gender Roles within the Boston Church of Christ, 1979-1989." Unpublished manuscript, last modified April 28, 2015. Microsoft Word file.

INDEX

Printed in the USA
CPSIA information can be obtained
at www.ICGtesting.com
LVHW022207201023
761678LV00029B/772/J